Healing to Harmony

Healing to Harmony

Solutions for Healthy Relationships in Recovery

Rena K.

Contents

Acknowledgments

"Thank you" seems like such an inadequate way to express the love and appreciation I feel for those who have been instrumental in bringing this dream to reality; my gratitude is profound:

Alcoholics Anonymous — I would like to humbly acknowledge my debt to A.A. The worst day of my life turned out to be the best day of my life;

Cole K. — My hero in life, who encourages me when I don't feel worthy;

Nina K. — Who knew me when I was drinking, loved me anyway, and is proud of me now;

Tommie D. — Who taught me unconditional love and shared her wisdom with me for more than 40 years;

Cyndi M. — Who shares her wisdom with me now;

Denise H. — Who unfailingly offered encouragement, support and brilliant ideas. She is the best editor and special friend one could ever have;

Janet F. — My dearest friend and cheerleader who has lived through these growing-up experiences with me for the last 45 years – we will continue this journey together;

Marty J. — Mentor, designer, and most of all, friend;

Andy C. — Who gave me the idea in the first place and whose knowledge and encouragement are priceless;

Pamela Workman — An unexpected blessing who has patiently walked me through every step of the book-making process;

Sarah Lahay — Who honored my indecisive ways and helped me anyway;

Lesley R. — Whose sense of humor and Apple skills saved my sanity;

The men and women who have completed this workshop, sometimes more than once! It is from you that I have gained more and more clarity about relationships and how and why they work;

The women I have sponsored, am sponsoring, and will sponsor. Because you give me the privilege of entering your lives in a meaningful way, I turn the spotlight on me, find out who I truthfully am, and revel in the growth opportunities! I am who I am today because of you.

And here's to you, Bill Allen!

I am blessed beyond measure. I thank you all; I love you all.

Introduction

THIS IS A WORKBOOK about relationships. Why did I write it, and why do you need it?

Remember your vision when you entered recovery, "Life will be different, and I will be happy and free in all areas of my life once I get out from under all this chaos!"

And so it is. If you work for it.

No one told you how much work you would have to do or what *kind of work* "real" sobriety entailed. But you were ready to grow, to be transformed.

And that's what this Workbook is about. It's why I wrote it and why you need it.

When I finally dragged myself into Alcoholics Anonymous in 1975, I discovered that I had the cart before the horse: I laid my problems at other people's feet and blamed them for the failure of almost all my relationships, especially romantic ones. "You need to change so I'll feel better!" was my perpetual cry.

I assumed that once I was sober, I would have perfect relationships, and we would all live happily ever after.

It didn't happen.

Sadly, in sobriety, I found I was having the same difficulties with relationships that I had experienced long before Alcoholics Anonymous and even before I had my first drink. Although I was sober, I still had trouble with family, friends, neighbors, clerks in department stores, other drivers, and sometimes even my cat annoyed me.

Maybe you have also experienced some of these problems in sobriety:

- Have you ever tried to discuss a problem with your dearly beloved and ended up shouting angrily at each other with no resolution to the problem? Or have you ever given each other the "Silent Treatment" for days?

- Have you ever had a boss or co-worker bully you, and you didn't know how to handle it, so you kept quiet and complained to others behind his back?

- Have you ever had someone angry with you, you can't stop thinking about it, and it ruined your whole day?

- Have you ever walked into a room and just knew they were talking about you, finding you insignificant?

- Have you ever felt uncomfortable because you have been asked to do something you don't want to do, and you don't know how to say "No," so you say "Yes" and have a resentment bigger than Texas?

I have. I've had all these situations happen – *in sobriety!*

Every encounter is a relationship. I have connections for a reason, a season, or a lifetime. If you have had the same disappointing experiences in sobriety as I have, this workbook may have your solutions. In it, you will learn how to *communicate*, not just talk, to *hear*, not just listen, to *forgive*, not just resent, to *love*, not just take hostages, and to be your authentic self.

I had to be in a lot of psychic pain before I would follow a sponsor's suggestions and incorporate the Twelve

Steps into my life. I had to be in even more emotional distress to be willing to even *look* at the Twelve Traditions of Alcoholics Anonymous. I thought of them as boring rules, and I didn't like rules!

I thought of myself as a relationship expert. After all, I had been married three times by the time I came to A.A. My sponsor pointed out that they had all ended in divorce, and the common denominator in all three was *me*. She told me the problem was that I didn't know *how* to have healthy relationships; I had learned from faulty role models who also didn't know how to have healthy relationships.

Remember the movie "28 Days," where the girl was told as she left the treatment center, "First get a houseplant and take care of it for a year. If it doesn't die, get a pet. If the pet thrives and is alive in a year, you can consider a relationship." In between the pet and the man, my sponsor inserted, "Learn to have healthy relationships with other women." I did as she suggested. Imagine! Women as friends!

When I was two years sober, I met the next "man of my dreams." We were the perfect A.A. couple: we never argued; we were always loving, kind, and well-dressed. If we disagreed, we would take a break, go to our respective homes, get back together, and never mention the issue or a possible solution. No one told us this was an unhealthy way to run a relationship. Bill and I dated for three years, and then we married. Before the ink was dry on our marriage certificate, we were ready to kill each other or head to divorce court. What had happened? Why had *he* changed from a loving, playful companion to a raging, annoying control freak?

I will share with you how we resolved these sober relationship problems using our Higher Powers, our sponsors, all Twelve Steps and Traditions, and relationship advice from experts, including some professional help. It took both of us to be 100% committed to the marriage, many attempts to spiritually change ourselves rather than each other, and many temporary setbacks. Still, we persevered. Slowly, ever so slowly, we worked toward a reasonably happy, healthy relationship.

Actually, every relationship changed and improved as I worked the Traditions into my daily interactions. *They didn't change; I did!* I use the Twelve Steps to live with *myself.* I use the Twelve Traditions to live with *us.* If applied to our personal lives, the Steps put our lives in order, not necessarily our relationships. How to live successfully with each other can be found in our Instruction Manual: the Traditions of Alcoholics Anonymous.

That's what this workbook is all about. I have presented "Living the Traditions in Relationships" many times. I have been told that this remarkable story of transformation could be helpful to others who are struggling with sober relationships and don't know why.

Now I've been asked to put this workshop into print, into a workbook.

Each person, couple, or group can create their own transformation. This workbook can be used independently or as part of an in-person or online group. This practical workbook encompasses almost fifty years of personal experiences of trial and error, correction and success. It also incorporates information from "Twelve Steps and Twelve Traditions" and proven recommendations from some real experts.

It's just that simple. So, welcome to the start of happy, healthy relationships.

P.S. *All* proceeds from the sale of this book will be donated equally to *Dr. Bob's House* in Akron, Ohio, *Stepping Stones* in New Bedford, New York, and *Wilson House* in East Dorset, Vermont.

Why Unity?

IN OUR BOOK Twelve Steps and Twelve Traditions, Tradition One states: Our common welfare should come first; personal recovery depends on A.A. Unity.

"The unity of Alcoholics Anonymous is the most cherished quality our society has. *We stay whole, or A.A. dies*."

I believe this applies to our individual relationships as well as our fellowship.

For *our* purposes, Tradition One could read: "In any relationship, whether it's for a reason, a season, or a lifetime, our common welfare comes first. ***Every* healthy relationship depends on unity.**"

I was not quite a year sober when my home group voted to make the last meeting of the month a Traditions meeting. I was dismayed. I didn't want to spend a whole hour talking about the rules of A.A. How boring! It *was* boring until my sober life started interfering with my serenity, then I began to see a connection. I found people, places, and things sometimes refused to bow to my greater wisdom. People often annoyed me! I definitely "suffered under the delusion that I could wrest satisfaction and happiness out of this world if I only managed well." I guess I wasn't managing well, *so I tried harder.*

I began to suspect the Big Book was right – *maybe I was a **little** bit at fault.* An undercurrent of dis-ease ran through my life: I had trouble with some personal relationships, couldn't control my emotional nature, and was vaguely unhappy and restless.

With my sponsor and meetings, I slowly began to see that my troubles were basically of my own making. Even in sobriety, I was still an extreme example of self-will run riot.

Strong words. And it would appear I couldn't change this on my own. I had to have God's help.

But there was a problem: I was not raised to believe in God. Through the spiritual experience of staying sober,

I came to believe there is a power greater than myself. I came to call this power "God" because that is an acceptable term in the Western world for this power. *It's just a word.* Webster defines "word" as "A speech sound that symbolizes and communicates meaning."

I came to believe there is only one God. I think he relates to us in different ways. My friend Lori says it this way, and this is how it makes sense to me:

There is only one me. My husband calls me sweetheart or honey. I have a daughter, and she calls me Mom. I have friends who call me by different nicknames.

All of them call me different names, and I have a different relationship with every one of them. There is no end to my love for each of them within that relationship.

Every one of them is a different relationship. *But there's only one me.* And I think that's the way it is with God. I believe there is just one God. Some people call him Jesus, some call him Buddha, some call him Allah, some call him the moon and the stars, and some call him the spirit of nature. *It's just a word.* And each person has a different relationship with that word. But there's only one God, and how we get to that higher power is as unique and individual as each of us.

That's what finally clicked for me. "God as you understand him." The beauty of our A.A. program is that each of us believes whatever we want to believe, and no one can say we're wrong.

So, I began a relationship with God. I did that just like I would do with anybody. I started having a conversation, and he started talking back to me. God speaks to me in a million ways. He talks to me through music, he talks to me through you, he talks to me through conversations at the next table, a book I'm reading, the birds singing early in the morning, the moon rising at night. *If I'm tuned in, I hear him.*

Over the years, we have developed quite a relationship, but there is still only one me and there is still only one God.

My sponsor suggested that the Steps were for **me**, the Traditions were for me and anybody else who appeared on my horizon! I began to pay attention to those Tradition meetings. I started to read the ***back half*** of our book "Twelve Steps and Twelve Traditions." I even read the comic book version of "The Traditions" with all the cute pictures. Only this time, I tried to apply what I learned to my daily, minute-to-minute life.

I found I could transfer the results of my practice in the A.A. rooms to the outside world.

Let's look at some definitions so we're all on the same page when we're talking about incorporating the Traditions in our relationships.

What **is** our common welfare? It is our well-being and our healthiness as a group, whether the group consists of one hundred or just two people.

What is unity? The dictionary defines unity as "wholeness, "harmony," "integrity," and "peace." The definition I like best is: "a whole or totality as combining all the parts into one." *The whole is greater than the sum of its parts*. Our well-being begins with the individual. Unity begins with the individual. Our success individually depends on the principle of unity.

So how does this apply to me, me, me?

All I had to do was look at my history for the answer. Bear with me because I have to share me with you, so you can see *why* I have had so many problems in relationships all my life and *why* the Steps and Traditions were the answer to all these problems.

A light bulb turned on when it hit me that **from my** *second* **drink of alcohol, I drank for unity.**

Before the **first** drink, I didn't know of the transformation that would take place. But *after* the first drink, I knew. Alcohol made me feel like I belonged, like I fit in. I had yearned for unity since I was a little girl. I didn't know that **unity** was what I was seeking. I just thought I was *lonely*. You and I may experience the feeling of loneliness differently, but I know *you* know what I mean when I talk of the loneliness, self-pity, and resentment we all feel.

I knew as a child that I was a misfit, an outsider. I remember secretly watching other people to figure out how I should act. I wore a mask to keep you from seeing the *real me*. I learned how to manipulate and lie outright to get out of trouble, to twist the truth, and to get what I wanted. I have no idea why I felt so unlovable. I was never told these things about myself; I just drew my own conclusions about me, about you, and about life. I was a fear-based child, sullen and withdrawn. I was defiant, self-reliant, and self-absorbed.

I felt I had to care for myself because no one else could or would. There was no God in my life – my parents didn't believe in God; they believed in money, property, and prestige. I blamed everyone else for my problems. I didn't know it, but I identified myself as a victim of life and the people in it. I cried, *"If you would only change to suit me, I'd feel better!"* I was a spectator in my own life.

All this by the time I was 7. By the time I was 7, I had put every character defect firmly in place. A character defect is just a way of dealing with the world. It was my orientation toward life.

I never took responsibility for my actions, never admitted a mistake, and was never aware of or responsible for my negative attitudes or self-defeating behaviors. I never saw anything from *your* point of view, only my own, and *I was always right*!

Everything was your fault! My *life* was your fault!

And this is the miserable woman I brought to Alcoholics Anonymous on October 16, 1975.

I firmly believed that I knew how to have successful relationships. After all, I'd been married three times by the time I came to you. My sponsor gently pointed out that every one of my marriages ended in divorce and that I was the common denominator in all three. When she suggested that I not date or make any major changes during the first year of sobriety, I was *horrified*. I didn't see the correlation between sobriety and dating: "I just came here to get sober," I whined. "That's what I'm talking about," she said. The clincher was this: "Besides, Rena, you are so sick only a sick man would be attracted to you! Why don't you get well, and *then* you can attract a healthy man?"

Somehow, I knew this was true. By the time I crawled into the doors of A.A., I knew there was more wrong with me than drinking alcohol. I just didn't know what it was.

In **relationships,** I always thought **my** only mistake was in choosing the wrong people: the wrong friends, the wrong employers, the wrong boyfriends, and the wrong husbands. When the relationship failed, **and it always did,** I believed it was because of *my* bad luck and *my* inability to find the right people. "Why does this always happen to me, me, me?"

Time after time, I would enter a new relationship with high hopes for living happily ever after, only to once again be bitterly disappointed, frustrated, and alone. Of course, I demanded "happily ever after," according to *my* definition. I never asked you what *your* definition was!

I was baffled. I saw happy relationships all around me, and I couldn't figure out why it had never happened to me.

This is the woman who wanted to jump into a new relationship in A.A. before the ink was dry on my membership card! This is the woman who heard her sponsor say, "Rena, you have to become a healthy woman before a healthy man will want to have anything to do with you."

This was the beginning of my awareness that *I* had a part in the success or failure of a relationship. It wasn't all your fault, after all.

Imagine my surprise when I was told that the problem was that I didn't know **how** to have a healthy relationship. It wasn't bad luck or bad choices; it was **bad information**. I had never been **taught** healthy relationship skills.

What?

This is where I started using the Traditions in my relationships, although I didn't call it that, I called it "*my sponsor made me.*"

She said I was to start slowly and learn **how** to have healthy relationships in other areas of my life before getting involved with another man. I always defined a relationship as having to do with some guy. What did she mean by *"relationships in other areas of my life"*?

If dating was out, what was left?

Oh no! My sponsor made me go to the Women's meeting every week!

How I hated it! While I knew that men were easy to manipulate, I believed women could see right through me to the unlovable, unlikeable person I thought I was. And the women's meeting was full of *women*!

I believe Alcoholics Anonymous is God's schoolroom for life lessons.

My "relationship education" began at that women's meeting. They made me a greeter! I told myself I was *shy* and shouldn't have to put myself out there. *I figured out later that "shy" is just another way of saying "self-centered."* I had to be friendly and welcome each woman with a smile. Imagine my surprise when they smiled back at me. My hostile defensiveness began to melt as I started to feel a sense of connectedness and unity and began to believe that I was included in it.

It made me feel warm and fuzzy all over.

I started to pay attention when someone said their husband was sick or their child was graduating from high school. I would write this information down after the meeting so that the next week, I could review my notes and remember to ask how the husband was doing and about the graduation. Slowly, as I became more comfortable, I became more willing to listen to other women's ideas, feelings, and opinions with an almost open mind. I began to share *my* thoughts, feelings, and opinions with some of these women. I began to let go of my "shyness," my sensitivity, my need to be right, and my feelings of superiority and inferiority.

Healing took place through my actions and my behavior.

When I was about three weeks sober, I heard a speaker say, *"I have to act my way into good thinking; I can't think my way into good acting."* I had no idea what this meant, but I felt it was important, so I wrote it down. I didn't know it then, but that concept was to become the foundation of my transformational change in A.A. For example, look at the *actions* I took as a greeter and how my thinking and feelings changed due to those actions that were **contrary** to *my* thinking and feelings!

Here's another example of acting my way into good thinking, of *incorporating the* **principle of unity** *into my life:*

It was the first time one of my home group members asked me to go out for ice cream with "the Gang" after the meeting. I didn't hear a word of that meeting because I was so preoccupied with myself:

> "What will I say? How should I act? Have I dressed appropriately? And *what grown-up eats ice cream anyway*? Ice cream is for kids' birthday parties! "

I fearfully took the *action* and went with the others for ice cream after the meeting. I discovered several important facts: I didn't do all the talking. The focus was on the group members and *general conversation,* not me, me, me. No one paid any attention to how I was dressed; it was all about the fellowship. I felt accepted by "the Gang." I felt the *spirit of unity* at that table. Everyone was equal, and everyone – **including me** – belonged. By the way, ice cream is definitely for grownups!

I was unaware of this transformation. It unconsciously took place one situation at a time. *I live my life forward but understand it backward.* In each situation, I stood at a turning point: I could choose to practice the principles of love and tolerance of others, or I could choose to be my old self-righteous, critical, demanding self. *With every decision I make, I move towards or away from a drink.*

I was learning how to have healthy relationships, although I wouldn't have called it that. I would have called it "**sobriety.**" And so it was. I joined that women's group and made it my home group. I began participating in the *"group conscious meetings."* held once a month and saw **the concept of unity** at work. I witnessed women able to "disagree without being disagreeable."

Believe me; my motives were not pure! I took the high road because *I wanted to fit in*, not because I wanted to *change*, and certainly not because I wanted to be loving and tolerant! But slowly, I began to fit into the women's meeting. *I even made a few friends, carefully practicing this newfound "love and tolerance" attitude on them.*

I continued to go out for ice cream with them after the meeting, then began to meet individual women for dinner before the meeting. I began to feel safe. I began to have a sense of belonging. I began to look fondly at the women who came into A.A. after I did. I could make them feel welcome because I remembered how I felt as a newcomer.

I knew somehow that I was *practicing the tradition of unity* in my relationships. I knew that even if I made mistakes, you wouldn't kick me out of A.A. I didn't realize

I was practicing the opposite of my fundamental problem of *self-centeredness.*

I was beginning to have that feeling of *belonging* I had yearned for all my life.

Here's an example *outside* the rooms of A.A. When I was about six months sober, I was in the bank waiting in line to cash a check. I began to get irritated that the line wasn't moving faster. "Don't they know who I am!" I was about to leave in disgust when suddenly, the thought came into my head that I was part of *this* group, too; I needed to practice the principle of **unity** in **all** my affairs. I asked God for patience; I relaxed and chatted with the woman in front of me in the line. It turns out she was impatient, too, and we laughed about it. She felt like I did! This was a **huge** step in recognizing the *connectedness* and the *similarities* we have as human beings. This was a lesson I could apply to *other* circumstances in my life. *My learning was cumulative!* I was including others in my universe. *I was no longer alone.* **Unity** was alive and well even *outside* the rooms of A.A. – *even in the bank!*

When I was two years sober, I met Bill – "**the one**" – at an A.A. meeting, and we started dating. We did not live together for the three years we dated; whenever we disagreed, he would retreat to his house, and I would retreat to mine. We would always come back together and never mention the disagreement. *We never resolved any conflict.* Then we married and shared the same house. Everything we had learned about sobriety went out the window as fear of losing control came in. *It was awful!* We were two babies sitting in our high chairs, banging on our trays, demanding our way, and insisting that the other was wrong, wrong, wrong! We were headed for disaster! We were a group of two who desperately needed help. But *each of us genuinely believed the fault lay with the other person!* We lived and judged each other by the *unspoken rules* we had learned as children in our different families. We each had a set-in-stone mindset about marriage, about the different roles each played – and guess what? They didn't always mesh! As a result, we both felt misunderstood and frustrated most of the time.

My sponsor gave me a copy of **"The Four Agreements"** by Don Miguel Ruiz. He has some interesting theories. The most fascinating part of the book for me at that time was his description of *The Domestication of Humans:* "Children are domesticated the same way we would domesticate a dog or a cat." He says that through this domestication, the information from the outside of us is conveyed to the inside of us, creating our whole belief system. Day by day, from our parents and siblings at home, at school, at church, and from television, we are taught how to live. Even when we're rebels, we learn what kind of behavior is acceptable and what is not. We have a whole concept of what the world is about. We learn to judge because we've been trained about "right" and "wrong." We become a carbon copy of Mama's beliefs, Daddy's beliefs, and society's beliefs. Eventually, we become something we're not in order to please those people, to reap *reward, and* avoid *punishment*. We become so well trained that we become our own domesticators – we don't need anyone to domesticate us. This is our TRUTH.

We punish ourselves when we don't live according to those beliefs and reward ourselves when we do. We base all our judgments on this truth, even our judgment of ourselves. Everything lives under the tyranny of this judge. Now, we become the Victim. We formed the image of perfection we wished to be in order to be good enough. We could never live up to this image, so we put on a mask and *pretended* to be perfect, rejecting who we really are, and becoming a victim of our self-imposed belief system. We reject ourselves. The victim carries the shame, the guilt, and the blame. "I'm not good enough, smart enough, pretty enough – I am not worthy of love."

All of this is based on a belief system we never chose to believe. These beliefs are so strong that, as adults, when we are exposed to new concepts and try to make our own decisions, we find that these beliefs still control our lives. I suffer, and all my relationships – every one of them – suffer.

In his letter on **emotional maturity**, Bill Wilson talks about our "expectations" becoming "demands." My Bill and I never discussed these misunderstandings and frustrations to find the root cause; *we blamed each other for how we felt.*

Just like the cavalry in the old movies, this is where *all the Traditions* came roaring into our *personal* lives as guides for achieving sane, healthy, loving relationships.

It took the Twelve Steps and the Twelve Traditions, two loving sponsors, a loving higher power, and much hard work on **both** our parts to change the destructive, self-centered *relationship patterns* we had unknowingly established as children. We found that *both* partners must act as a group of two, and we must be 100% committed to the *unity of the relationship.*

What was different? I was sober and trying to live by A.A.'s principles: No more disposable relationships when things didn't go my way!

Just as in an A.A. group, our group of two had to be willing to work for harmony. At five and nine years sober, Bill and I knew *intellectually* that we needed to change our attitudes and actions but had no clue **how** to do that. I had to learn acceptance, tolerance, and love the same way I learned it in the "My Sponsor Made Me" much-feared women's group, in the bank situation when I was new to Alcoholics Anonymous, and in several situations I had encountered in my first two years of sobriety *before* I met Bill. This seemed overwhelming! The wisdom of my sponsor when I was a newcomer suddenly made sense. My problem was that although I knew how to have a relationship, I didn't know how to have a ***healthy*** relationship. It wasn't bad luck or bad choices; it was ***bad information*** I had learned from unhealthy role models as a child. Did she mean I would have to unlearn and relearn *everything* I thought I knew about relationships with men, too? The answer was "Yes."

This was not an easy task. I had to learn that, in any group, we're on the *same team!* If my motive is to win at any cost, someone else must lose. **Sadly, I discovered that one of my problems in relationships with everyone was my need always to be right and in control.** Only my need to stay sober was greater than my need to be right and in control. I knew I wouldn't stay married if I didn't change. It's just that I had no idea **how**, **where**, and **what** I would need to change.

This is what we'll be talking about in the following eleven Traditions.

Along with our *self-centeredness*, our problems are defined by **unconscious** Rules and Roles. We all have de-lusions of control that *we don't think about* till we get into so much pain that we will either fight, flee, or change. Once we become aware of the underlying "truths," we can examine them, evaluate them, and decide on their usefulness *today*. **"Uncover, discover, discard,"** we say in A.A.

Thank God we have sponsors and a day-at-a-time program! I learned that in the morning, I could ask God to remove the character defect of *self-centered fear* just for today and then **act as if he had.**

Pausing when agitated or doubtful became one of the most important tools in my new relationship toolbox. **The pause isn't me waiting for God to catch up; the pause is God!** Sometimes, I have to ask God to help me "pause" 100 times during the day! One hundred times a day, I remind myself that I am no longer running the show, and I say, "Thy will be done." Sometimes, I say it through gritted teeth, *but I say it*. My goal is to be free from the *bondage of self* and the pain this bondage creates.

It was so hard to keep the critical spotlight on *me*. It was so much easier and more comfortable to find fault with Bill and want *him* to change so I'd feel better. No, *I had to change* **my attitude** *so I would feel better*. **This shift in focus put the control of me back** *inside* **of me.** Imagine that! I didn't have to wait for him to change so I'd feel better. **That is a** *victim attitude* that placed control of me directly into his hands! I began to see that I had given control of myself to *anything* and *everything* outside myself since I was a child, although I had not seen it that way.

Did I take everything personally? Of course I did! As a self-centered individual, it was my *job* to know that everything was about me, me, me. Everything was intended for and directed at **me**. I had seen myself as a powerless victim. The 12 x 12 states unequivocally, ***"It is a spiritual axiom that every time [I] am disturbed, no matter what the cause, there is something wrong with [me]."*** I found that I felt better as soon as my attitude changed from self-centeredness to one of God-centeredness, unity, and love.

Isn't that why I put alcohol inside of me – to feel better? *Now I was learning to put Alcoholics Anonymous inside of me to feel better*! Each time Bill did something that was "wrong" (loading the dishwasher, driving the car, folding the towels, brushing his teeth), I would get upset and want to correct him, to tell him how to do it "right." My sponsor taught me to ask myself, "Where did I get the idea of what was right? Is it my parents? Were they right? Do I want to base my life on my alcoholic parents' beliefs?"

Was I misinformed by the misinformed? How important is it, anyway? These are unhealthy *control issues*, folks, which could ruin my marriage and cause a divorce!

We argued – **oh my!** Of course, we called them "discussions." We had no idea how to disagree without being disagreeable! Very frustrating! And non-productive! Just like when we were dating, we never *resolved* anything, although now we were trying to address our disagreements, sometimes, *at the top of our lungs*! Our sponsors taught us about "**Fair Fighting.**" It was probably one of the most important skills we learned (much more about these techniques later – google it). Fair Fighting gave us *specific* instructions about how to argue and achieve positive results without killing each other. Imagine our surprise when we discovered we had no idea **how** to **communicate** in a healthy way. I used the manipulative, underhanded methods I learned from my mother; Bill used the power-driven, angry mode of his father. No wonder we would end each *"discussion"* frustrated and resentful, with no solution for the original problem.

Our sponsors gave us a specific assignment: how we *hated* it in the beginning! But...*our sponsors made us do it. Every night,* we had to sit knee to knee, holding hands, reciting the serenity prayer out loud, and inviting God into our discussion. *Then* we could begin to talk, taking turns and ***not interrupting***. We had to say, "I feel a certain way," not "You made me feel a certain way," because that is a lie. No one can make me feel anything! *I* generate my feelings! Think about it. When someone speaks to me, I always have a *choice* in how I interpret those words. My old way was usually hostile and defensive. ***What's your old way?***

Conflict inevitably happens in every relationship. For many of us, it creates significant anxiety and discomfort, but if handled appropriately, conflict can strengthen relationships and improve our understanding of each other. When poorly managed, conflict can result in severed relationships, broken friendships, and bitter hostility.

Here are just some of the **ground rules** our sponsors gave us:

- Remain calm throughout the discussion
- Be specific about what is bothering you
- Deal with only one issue at a time
- Leave the past in the past; don't bring up past sins
- Avoid accusations
- Don't generalize
- Avoid clamming up; avoid the silent treatment

Before we began our discussion about whatever issue was currently on the table, Bill and I learned to talk about what these **ground rules** meant to each of us. This way, we would each clearly understand how the other felt.

*We learned that our goal was not to "win" but to find a **mutually** satisfying and peaceful solution to any problem.*

We began to find solutions to our problems rather than sticking with the problems as we had in the past. What a concept!

We learned it wasn't just about Bill and me. There was a bigger picture!

Any two or more people constitute a group, whether in a marriage, with a child, a friend, an associate at work, a clerk in a grocery store, or the people in the car ahead of me driving way too slowly. No matter how fleeting, a relationship is formed, at least in my head, and must be navigated. *I get to choose how I operate in every encounter.*

What happens if I mishandle a "relationship"?

I was about **20** years sober when this example of *how not to do it right* reared its ugly head: I was in a department store with a friend and saw a little clock I wanted. The only clerk in the store was on the phone (chatting with a friend, I was sure). I waited and waited, growing more impatient, till she finally got off the phone. *So now we're a group of two*, with my friend looking on. I angrily and arrogantly told her what I thought of her behavior and walked out of the store. Within 30 seconds, I turned around, walked back into the store, and apologized for *my* bad behavior. I even bought the clock!

I left the store feeling great. I used the principle of *unity* to recover from ego-driven self-centeredness and promote harmony in our little group of two in the department store. After I made my amends, I loved that clerk! The "we" was more important than the "you" or the "I."

It was the next right thing to do right!

By the way, I found out later that I was a good example of A.A. *in living color* to the sober friend who was with me that day.

I benefit from mutual, unified support by prioritizing our little group's shared interests. As in an A.A. group, each member is heard and respected, but our common welfare must come first. This is especially true in close relationships: partners, women I sponsor, my sponsor, friends, children, parents, other relatives, or co-workers—people who are in our lives on a long-term basis.

In the past, I had always taken *hostages*. I saw other people only in terms of their value to *me* and what they could do for *me*. They were one-dimensional, **cardboard** actors on *my* stage who were supposed to recite *my* lines. Didn't they know this? It never occurred to me that *I was a user of people* – how could that be when I was such a victim? My problems were all **their** fault anyway. I used people for my purposes and discarded them like yesterday's trash. I would have been astounded if someone had told me I had hurt people – didn't they know what *they* had done to *me, me, me*?

Sober and working the Steps and Traditions into my life, I could look back at my interactions with my parents, my daughter, boyfriends, husbands, friends, and co-workers and see that I had indeed roared like a tornado through their lives.

Living *in* the Twelve Traditions determines the *quality* of my life. My *behavior*, not my thoughts, feelings, or beliefs, dictates the healthiness of my relationships, whether for a lifetime or ten minutes.

Whether you are a newcomer to A.A., an old timer in A.A., or a non-alcoholic married to a sober alcoholic, *we are all on a path of change.* We are all being transformed from *self*-centered to *other*-centered. Some say we are transformed from self-centered to God-centered, but what's in a name – it's the idea that counts!

We all have to start from where we are; we can't start from anywhere else! The path does get easier as long as we *repetitively* practice these principles on a situational, daily, real-life basis. As you will see, each of the Traditions explains *one specific way* to protect the *Unity* of the fellowship and the group. **This applies to *individual* relationships as well**. The First Tradition is only the beginning. We have just begun to scratch the surface, folks!

I can't wait to tell you of the lessons we learned about the *Second* Tradition! "*Our leaders are but trusted servants.*"

You can *imagine* what it was for two self-willed drunks to deal with *this* concept, separately or together! In the following Traditions, we will explore different *manifestation*s of *unity* while learning how to uncover, discover, and discard our old ideas about how to do life so we can develop and cherish happy, loving, and healthy relationships.

Chapter One

Questions from Tradition One

1. *How do I define unity in a relationship?*

2. *How have I come to believe that sometimes I don't know how to have healthy relationships? Do I think that I can learn this skill?*

3. *Am I flexible? What does that mean?*

4. *How healthy are my communication skills? Who initially taught me those skills? Are they valid today? If they are not valid, what will I replace them with?*

5. *How are my listening skills? Do I formulate my response while the other person is talking, or do I really listen?*

6. *How am I able to express my thoughts and feelings in a non-confrontational, loving way?*

7. *Can I listen to another's thoughts and feelings without becoming defensive and argumentative? How can I improve my attitude?*

8. *Am I outgrowing my sensitivity? (Remember, our literature says it takes some of us a long time to overcome this aspect of our emotional immaturity!) Or is it always about me, me, me? How can I change this thinking?*

9. *Am I outgrowing my need to be right, or do I always need to win? How can I change this thinking?*

10. *How have I come to believe that I must act my way into good thinking and can't think my way into good acting?*

11. *Do I try to promote harmony and unity in all my relationships, no matter how fleeting they might be?*

12. *Do I remember to pause when agitated or doubtful? Do I recognize agitation or doubt, or am I just uncomfortable because I want my way and am willing to go to any lengths to get it? How can I change this thinking?*

13. *Do I keep the spotlight on me when I'm upset, or do I focus on the faults of others and demand they change so I'll feel better? How can I change this thinking?*

14. *Am I still viewing myself as a "victim" of life? Do I blame others? Why? What do I get out of being a victim? What can I do to change this thinking?*

15. *Am I still holding onto my "old ideas" of right and wrong in relationships (and everything else) based on the beliefs I was taught as a child? (Remember "The Domestication of Children" from The Four Agreements by Don Miguel Ruiz? How can I change this thinking?)*

16. *How can I bring the element of unity into my relationships?*

17. *Do I discuss all these issues with my sponsor or another trusted spiritual advisor? Two heads are always better than one!*

Fair Fighting

There are lots of resources available out there. Our favorite turned out to be Fair Fighting. (SEE APPENDIX)

First, we made a copy of the fair fighting rules so each person would have that list and refer to it when "discussing" a problem. (Soon, we no longer needed the paper; we had internally incorporated the ground rules!).

Then, we discussed what the ground rules meant to each of us so we'd be on the same page.

Here are some of the questions we ask ourselves about Fair Fighting:

1. *Are we learning and incorporating the ground rules for "fair fighting" into our relationships?*

2. *Do we remain calm throughout any discussion?*

3. *Do we describe exactly what is bothering us – are we specific?*

4. *Do we avoid clamming up or the silent treatment? (That is The #1 relationship killer—it destroys all possibilities of communicating.)*

5. *Do we deal with only one issue at a time?*

6. *Do we leave the past in the past? Do we avoid bringing up past issues?*

7. *Do we avoid accusations?*

8. *Do we avoid generalizations?*

These are just some of the ways we can change our old, ineffective patterns of interacting into new, goal-oriented, win-win relationships. They are all based on the principle of the First Tradition in relationships: the principle of unity.

Protecting Unity!

Tradition Two states: For our group purpose, there is but one ultimate authority – a loving God as He may express himself in our group conscience. Our leaders are but trusted servants; they do not govern.

For our purposes, Tradition Two could read: There is but one authority in any relationship, a **loving** God as he may express himself in the group's conscience. Each person in the relationship is God's trusted servant – one person does not govern.

The Second Tradition gets me out of the way!

Who's the boss? Any relationship is unhealthy when one person dominates it. If they impose an attitude of "being boss, "resentments flourish! The dominant one becomes responsible for the relationship's growth, or lack of growth, and the other partner begins to feel victimized. Participation as equals in any relationship is vital to its growth. When both are trusted servants, harmony is achieved. A loving God can enter when we're courteous and "equal."

Sounds pretty good, doesn't it? But what happens when the person is self-centered, not God or other-centered?

Our Big Book says our troubles center in our minds rather than our bodies.

What does this mean?

My own story before I came to A.A. is a good example of what I mean. Chaos ruled my life, although I didn't know this. The external circumstances of my life didn't shape me; my *thoughts* about those circumstances and my *reactions* to those thoughts are what shaped me. I lived in reaction to my instincts, feelings, obsessions, and impulses. – all limited and fueled by a life run on self-will.

Alcoholics Anonymous gives me a set of positive principles that shape my relationship with God, my relationship with you, and my relationship with me.

Bear with me. You may be saying, "This isn't a speaker meeting! What does her childhood have to do with Traditions and relationships?"

Everything!

I'm telling you my story to illustrate that we don't enter any relationship with a clean slate—we come bearing baggage, and it profoundly affects every interaction we have.

As I was growing up, I learned how to navigate relationships through the example of my parents. Where else was I going to learn it? I watched their behavior and the way they treated each other. I watched how they treated their friends.

They taught me how to be a human, and their beliefs were firmly entrenched in me by the time I was 5 or 6 years old.

Through *my* perception, interpretation, and thinking, I made decisions about life and how to live it. I observed, learned, and perfected their techniques. In my experience, the man was loud and overpowering, and the woman had to manipulate her way around him, winning every time. My parents used these techniques to manage and control each other, the world, and me.

I knew no other way, so I used these techniques to manipulate and control others. I used this passive-aggressive behavior despite the failed personal relationships it generated. It was my approach to life. I really believed that if my efforts at control didn't work the first time, I should try harder. It never occurred to me to try *different*.

By the way, they were both high-functioning alcoholics, so you have to know *their* thinking was off, too!

Early on, I realized that successful manipulation brought with it a certain contempt for the man and his "leadership" and a smug feeling of superiority in me. My manipulation also brought about a sense of shame because I believed that I couldn't just be myself and be okay, that I had to hide the real me behind a mask of exploitation, just like my mother did. I began to feel that I didn't measure up — *I was never enough.*

So this was how I thought about myself all my life. I covered it with arrogance and makeup and never let anybody see the real me, the inadequate me. Manipulation sometimes works as a tool to get my way, but feeling that I have to manipulate others because I'm not good enough does terrible things to my self-esteem. There was no equality anywhere in my life. I was either above or below everyone.

To justify all this, I had to find fault with everyone else. I became very good at blaming. If it was not my fault, I could still be superior! It's funny, isn't it, that I felt I had to be perfect to avoid feeling worthless. This became an enormously time-consuming job, appearing perfect at all times in all ways. I was completely unaware of any of this, of course. I wonder how many other perfectionists feel the same way for the same reason.

Remember, this was *my* perception, which I incorporated as a set of absolute beliefs that I carried with me into all my relationships and into sobriety.

Our Big Book says our problem centers in our minds rather than our bodies. My story is a good example of that. My life takes place between my ears – in my thinking. My addictive thinking is what is behind my unmanageability. It's a perception problem.

This is the woman I brought to Alcoholics Anonymous.

My low self-esteem was even lower because of my behavior during my drinking days. I was a mess!

At the beginning of my sobriety, I didn't have too much trouble with these "old ideas" in dealing with people. My relationships consisted of *acquaintances* when I was new to A.A. Usually, these friendships were formed in the dreaded women's meeting I told you about. These relationships were shallow, undemanding, and forgiving. But I was learning how to be a friend for the first time in my life.

And how was I doing this? Why, by watching you, of course. In the same way I had watched my parents for instructions on life, I watched sober winners in A.A. to learn how to live a truly sober life and have healthy relationships.

Slowly, I began to see myself as an equal to you. As I worked with my sponsor and lived my life, I began to discover and *re-examine* my attitudes and beliefs about people. Before, if I stayed in one place long enough to form a friendship, it was always about how *you* could be a friend to *me*. It was always about *me, me, me*.

I had always looked at love the same way: how do *you* love *me*? What are you doing for me that shows me you love me? That was my question, my focus, and my criteria for "love." It never occurred to me to wonder how *I* was doing in the "love" department. The prayer of Saint Francis was not even on my radar!

I told you about the movie "28 Days," where a newly sober young woman was told as she left treatment *not* to go looking for a man. She was told to get a houseplant first. If the houseplant survived, she could get a pet. If the pet survived, she could perhaps incorporate a friend into her life. If she could have an ongoing, mutual relationship with a friend, then and only then could she even *think* about adding a man into her life. Good advice. I always thought I just needed to *find* the right person – I didn't know I had to *be* the right person.

Speaking of movies, when I think about the movies I saw and the books I read, it was always the same story: Boy meets girl; they fall in love, and a bunch of misunderstandings occur that they resolve with a kiss and a song. They get married, and they live happily ever after. This is one of the most dangerous sentences ever written – "*they lived happily ever after.*" Growing up, I thought that was the way it would be and *should* be. And it wasn't. By the time I got to A.A., I had been married and divorced three times. In each marriage, I thought *love* would make all my problems disappear, these men would make me whole, and our relationship would only get better and better simply because we "tied the knot." We were unaware of the unconscious rules and roles we grew up with. While we assumed our rules and roles were identical, they didn't even come close! We each blamed the other and cashed in our chips!

Here's a story that illustrates another way of looking at love:

"An old man says to a young man, 'Why are you eating that fish?' The young man says, 'Because I love fish.' 'Oh, you love fish. That's why you took it out of the water, killed it, and boiled it. Don't tell me you love the fish; you love yourself, and the fish tastes good to you; you took it out of the water, killed it, and boiled it.' So much of what is called love is fish love. And so, a young couple falls in love. A young man and a young woman, they fall in love. What does that mean?

That means he saw in this woman someone he felt could provide *him* with all his physical and emotional needs. And she saw the same thing in this man – here was somebody who could provide all *her* physical and emotional needs. But each one is looking out for their *own* needs; it's not love for the other. No, the other person becomes a vehicle for my gratification. Too much of what is called love is fish love. Love is not about what I'm going to *get* but what I'm going to *give*."

The only requirement for a loving, healthy relationship is a desire to be in a loving, healthy relationship and to behave in a manner that reflects that desire. I have to do to be. And that's one of the most profound things I'll ever say: **I must do to be**.

It is a testament to Alcoholics Anonymous and good sponsorship that today, I still have some of those friends I made early in sobriety. We have been sober for over 40 years, and I cherish each relationship. We have each made an effort to stay connected because the relationship is meaningful enough to take the *action* of staying connected on a reasonably regular basis. When they say you have to "work" on the relationship, they mean it. No matter how inconvenient or time-consuming, if the connection is precious, we will take the time and attention to keep connected. I've sponsored Janet for more than 40 years. We get together several times a year – by design. Each time we meet, it's as if we saw each other yesterday because we've kept connected *between* visits. With the advent of Zoom, we visit each other every week!

Let's go back to 1975 when I was a newcomer: I reluctantly took my sponsor's suggestion and didn't date or get emotionally involved with a man the first year.

I started dating Bill in my second year of sobriety; we rarely had any problems because we never addressed anything. We were courteous and on our best behavior until we married three years later. *I wish I'd known about the fish story at that time.* We each immediately retreated into massive, self-centered control mode. We became two babies who climbed up into their high chairs, demanded their way, and insisted the other person was wrong, wrong, wrong about everything!

What was our problem? What had happened to the two people who loved each other enough to pledge their undying love in a legal ceremony in front of God and their friends? Had we made a terrible mistake? No, through our sponsors and much hard work, we found out it meant that **we had prepared for a wedding but hadn't prepared for our marriage.** It never occurred to us that "love" means different things to different people based on the rules and roles we each bring to the relationship which were based on the "old ideas" we discussed earlier. ROLES AND RULES. This disconnect caused terrible tensions between the two of us. At this point, our sponsors introduced us to the Traditions. I wrote about the First Tradition in our last chapter. The Second Tradition talks about "trusted servants." What does that mean? It talks about "a loving God." What does *that* mean to us? Trusted servants sound like some kind of humility, which we both thought of as "humiliation." What is a loving God? Are we supposed to love like that? Then came the big question: ***How do we do that?*** How do we turn from the shouting, angry, hurtful idiots that we were into a loving, unified couple?

We learned we had conflicting, unspoken rules and roles regarding the marriage relationship. His childhood learning about relationships had been quite different from mine. He had grown up watching a quiet, dominant father and a submissive mother. I had grown up learning about relationships by watching a loud, dominant father who always gave in to my quiet, manipulative mother. Bill resisted my manipulative ways, and I defended my position. Based on our backgrounds, we were both right: I was right for me, and he was right for him.

Thankfully, we had each made a 100% commitment to our marriage. So now, what to do, what to do?

If we wanted to find harmony and have a healthy relationship, we needed to find mutually agreed-upon values based on the Principles of A.A.

We couldn't see the real problem at that time, so we were confused, angry, hurt, and very stubborn! Slowly, usually painfully, we began to follow instructions from our sponsors. We examined and discussed our respective values and convictions to find mutually agreed-upon *compromises*.

Once we had acknowledged that the only person we could change was ourselves, not each other, the road got a little smoother. But what were we to change? We began to acknowledge that we wanted a loving God to be the absolute authority in our lives.

Remember that all-important attitude adjustment I learned when I first got sober? ***I have to act my way into good thinking; I can't think my way into good acting***. It certainly applied here! Our **actions** had to be *contrary* to how each of us **felt**. We learned that our changed *actions* would change how we *think*, which in turn would change how we *felt*.

We began to have dinners with our sponsors so we could talk in a neutral atmosphere. We met at a restaurant, so we ***had*** to be polite to each other and to them. We would discuss our differences with them while they acted as referees. Sometimes, I would leave those dinners pouting, feeling my sponsor was on "his" side. But we were really uncovering and discovering that our problems were in the baggage we each brought to the relationship. We began to look at our "old ideas" about relationships. We asked ourselves, "Where did these ideas come from?" "Are these *my* beliefs or my parent's beliefs?" "What do I believe, and what kind of relationship do I want?"

Our reference point was always the Twelve Steps and Twelve Traditions. Because of our commitment to A.A. and each other, we started to let go of our old ideas and learned how to form new ones as partners, not adversaries.

If I turn over to the God of my understanding everything that happens this day in both my inside and the outside world, I give up my right to criticize or complain about anyone or anything for the rest of this day. Blaming and fault-finding are no longer an option – *for today!* This attitude helps me stay inside my own hula hoop and keeps me centered in *myself* rather than *you.*

Marital sobriety is easier to maintain if harmony in the home is more important than the desire to convince the other person they are wrong, and you are right.

I'll never forget the first time I looked at myself as the problem rather than Bill. My sponsor met me early one morning before she went to work. (How's *that* for unselfishness?). I was so upset – *"Maybe I'm a little bit at fault in some of this,"* I grudgingly said that morning.

"Great," she said. "Now you don't have to wait for him to change, so you'll feel better!" "***What do you want to do about it?***" She always put the responsibility for my happiness back on me rather than in someone else's hands. That way, I can do something about it. If it's in someone else's hands, I am indeed powerless! I discovered I had always put the keys to my happiness in someone else's pocket.

I began to look at my side of the street and became aware of some of the self-centeredness in my attitude and actions. I say "some" because, for me, nothing is revealed in its entirety. I have a slow, educational variety of spiritual awakenings. It is the peeling of the onion, I'm told. Do you know what happens when you peel an onion? You cry! And I did. Some of those tears were tears of hope, knowing that instead of sticking with the problem, I could move on to the solution.

Bill and I began to see, believe, and practice Tradition Two. We became a group of four – Bill and his higher power, me and mine. When I incorporated my loving God into my mix, *everything changed*. It changed mainly because I stopped trying to convert Bill to suit me and began to ask my God to transform me. I had to "see that my relationship with God was right," and I would be right. It was a spiritual thing, of course!

My job is to find and examine my motives, do the next right thing, and take the next right action. If my motive comes from love, it is always a good motive. If I leave the **results** up to the God of my understanding, things usually turn out better than I could have planned. Isn't that true for you, too?

51

I determine my attitude; my God determines reality and the results of my actions. I have very little to do with the outcome.

Tradition Two gets me out of the way.

I began to let go of always having to be right. I began to let go of the *illusion* of control. I realized my life is unmanageable by *me*, so why would I think I can manage *yours?* (This attitude is also crucial in sponsorship!). Becoming aware of this in my marriage meant I had to stop judging and criticizing Bill. I even learned how to give up my defensive ways and apologize when I was wrong!

I was no longer the A.A. police. When I was five years sober, this was especially difficult because I knew all the answers. I had absorbed enough of the Big Book and Twelve Steps and Twelve Traditions that I could spit it out on command. I knew what was right and wrong in A.A. and didn't hesitate to correct Bill or anyone else. Of course, I believed I knew what was right and wrong in all the other areas of your life as well! It was hard not to be a "bleeding deacon" at five years sober.

I became convinced that while I might be technically correct, I was spiritually wrong! My sponsor showed me how to really listen to Bill and to let go of the need to "fix" him. She said that's a control issue, cleverly disguised as being "helpful."

I began to talk to Bill about my real, intimate feelings despite my fear of appearing vulnerable. In my hostile world, vulnerable meant capable of being physically or emotionally wounded, exposed, or unprotected. Remember, my underlying core belief was that *I was worthless unless I was perfect*. Slowly and carefully, I began to let Bill see who I was, and he let me know who he really was. **"Intimacy is sharing from the heart without being judged."** I read that somewhere. Bill and I became intimate in a way I'd never known before despite all those marriages!

I stopped taking everything that happened as a personal affront. Finally, I began to see that the faults I objected to in Bill were usually the faults I disliked in myself. "If you spot it, you got it."

Saint Francis' prayer became my "owner's manual"— my *directions for living*. "What can I bring to the situation, not what can I get out of it?" became my attitude. It wasn't always about me, me, me!

Even though Saint Francis was not an alcoholic, Step Eleven in The Twelve and Twelve says, "He did, like us, go through the emotional wringer. And as he came out the other side of that painful experience, this prayer was his expression of what he could then see, feel, and wish to become:"

"Lord, make me a channel of your peace –
that where there is hatred, I may bring love –
that where there is wrong, I may bring the spirit
of forgiveness – that where there is discord,
I may bring harmony – that where there is error,
I may bring truth – that where there is doubt,
I may bring faith – that where there is despair,
I may bring hope – that where there are
shadows, I may bring light – that where there is
sadness, I may bring joy. Lord, grant that I may
seek rather to comfort than to be comforted –
to understand than to be understood –
to love than to be loved.
For it is by self-forgetting that one finds.
It is by forgiving that one is forgiven. It is by
dying that one awakens to eternal life.
Amen"

I loved it when I first read this prayer – until I got to that last sentence. I had a lot of trouble with having to die before I experienced all these goodies Saint Francis mentions. Then I realized he meant that I had to die to *self*: "Above everything, we alcoholics must be rid of this selfishness. We must, or it kills us! "Relieve me of the bondage of self." Saint

Francis was talking about the *symbolic* death of the false ego, not actual death.

"What can I bring to the situation, not what can I get out of it?" became a spiritual goal. I sought to love, comfort, and understand rather than to be loved, comforted, or understood. The most beautiful things began to happen: these values became a goal for *all* my relationships, not just the one I had with Bill (of course, it is always easier to be courteous to the stranger in the grocery store than to my ever-present husband at home!). I slowly became able to practice *healthy* relationships with others who came into my life, no matter how deep or fleeting the encounter was. I say "practice" because that is what it is. The only aspect of the A.A. program I've gotten 100% right is the not drinking thing, and that took a minute!

Looking back, I see I had begun this practice as a newcomer and later in the women's group. Without even knowing it, I had started to believe and practice Saint Francis prayer with others in the rooms of A.A. Now I began to practice it outside of A.A.– with my family, in the bank, the grocery store, with people ahead of me who drove too slowly –everyone I met.

There were no exceptions. *"Love and tolerance of others is our code."*

"Practice" means *repetition*, the key to living the A.A. way of life and letting go of my former controlling, judgmental way of dealing with life and everyone in it.

I began to *want* to be a trusted servant everywhere, not just in my home group of Alcoholics Anonymous. Love and service *is* the point. The rewards for adopting this attitude and behavior had instant results. Bill and I learned to discuss our differences *somewhat* calmly (without the presence of sponsors as referees).

Our sponsors had given us some *exact* instructions, and for a long time, we practiced this every night:

We sat knee to knee, held hands, and said the Serenity Prayer *out loud* before we began. *Out loud*, we invited God into our discussions. We adopted rule 62: we stopped taking ourselves so damned seriously. We even learned to laugh at some of our old beliefs about relationships.

Healthy marriages have three things in common:

- *A commitment to the spiritual and emotional growth of one's partner.* If they are alcoholics, this is demonstrated when both partners go to A.A.

- *A commitment to learning and practicing communication skills.* There are books and workshops on improving communication. Nothing beats talking to a wise sponsor about communication problems. When Bill and I were having dinner with our sponsors, we were learning how to communicate more effectively. They were the referees while we attempted to talk from the heart.

- *A commitment to resolve conflicts creatively.* We had a problem with this one. The Big Book says, "We ceased fighting anyone or anything," but some days, we severely annoyed each other. We were learning to deal with our conflicts without becoming aggressive or defensive. We were learning how to respond rather than react.

That phenomenon is examined in detail in other Traditions. I tended towards being the "react" persona when I first began this A.A. adventure.

When the Second Tradition is practiced, humility can exist because God is the loving authority, not one person. No partner has the right to decide what is suitable for both of us, and no partner has the right to speak for the other without consulting the other. We slowly became equal partners. Our partnership was greater than the sum of its parts.

It's easy to be in the Second Tradition, God-conscious and spiritual when I'm at home alone, kneeling beside my bed and saying my prayers. It is another thing when I leave my house and face the world. It is too easy to forget about God, get back in the driver's seat, and direct my day. Then, halfway through the day, I'd be in some *self-imposed dilemma*, and I would remember, "Oh yeah, I just turned my life and will back over to the care of *me*. How is that working out?" I began to wear what I call a "God ring" because of an experience I had in a grocery store. Standing at the checkout counter, I was slow in finding the correct change to pay the cashier. I became annoyed at myself because I was taking too long and thought I was inconveniencing the woman in line behind me. Then I became annoyed at *that* woman for making me feel inadequate! I saw the absurdity of my thinking – *this nonsense was all in my head!* I decided I needed a "God reminder." The ring is a gimmick to keep me God-conscious throughout the day. It is a ring I'm not used to wearing – so I am constantly aware of it. This is my signal: to stay in touch with God while doing mundane things: going to the grocery store, talking with a woman I sponsor, driving in heavy traffic, and even at the dentist. *God is the loving authority in my life.* It's incredible how effective this awareness becomes. It reminds me that I am *carrying* the message; I'm not the message itself. I am the vessel, not the well.

I created another "God nudge." I had a heavy foot when it came to driving and was always in a hurry. I even put a bumper sticker on the back of my car. It read: "*This too shall pass*." I decided to see if saying, "Thank you, God," at every red light would help my impatience. It did, and it does. Initially, I had to tell myself that the red light was God protecting me from an accident that was about to happen farther down the road. Now it's just another reminder of my gratitude for a second chance at life, having nothing to do with a potential "accident." By the way, I took that bumper sticker off my car.

How is *this* for being technologically up-to-date? I have alarms on my cell phone and watch that sound at different times of the day with messages reminding me that God loves me and is now running my show!

My efforts to change my negative, self-centered attitude through changing my *behavior* ultimately changes how I think and feel. My friend Jennifer says, "I know God is going to give me a wonderful day as soon as I change my attitude."

The Second Tradition gets me out of the way.

I am no longer an ant floating on a log, thinking I am steering the log!

When I started dating again, I never had a romantic relationship with a man who wasn't in A.A., so I've had *no* experience with a non-alcoholic *romantic* relationship, but I know that *principles* are universal, permanent, and fit everybody.

I also know that a lot of material is available for learning better communication skills, listening skills, and so on. As two sober alcoholics, Bill and I learned and accepted some **ground rules** that worked for us as two card-carrying members of Alcoholics Anonymous:

- We learned we couldn't belong to the same home group and would only occasionally go to a Speaker Meeting together. This is because we each needed to maintain our program as *individuals*. When we were in an A.A. meeting, our focus needed to be on the *meeting* and not on each other. If we were in the same discussion meeting, we would analyze what the other said or didn't say, and then we would voice our "constructive criticism" on the drive home.

- We learned not to call each other's sponsor and "tattle." Not that they would have put up with that!

- We learned *never* to sponsor each other.

- We learned not to tell each other to "call your sponsor," which is another way of saying, "You are crazy, and your sponsor will straighten you out." And "I am superior to you because I'm sane, and you're not."

Sobriety is a life-and-death matter, and we can't play around with it.

We respected each other's program and the right to live the Alcoholics Anonymous program *individually*. The interpretation of the program was between Bill, his sponsor, and God as he understood him. The same was true for me. We continued to pray together. We learned to cherish each other.

These same attitudes about autonomy apply whether one, both, or neither is in a recovery program. These are just some techniques for how to have a healthy, happy relationship.

I can think of nothing more important in a relationship than the support of my partner's self-esteem. One way to accomplish this is to acknowledge their importance. I could only do this through my actions. I showed Bill he was important by getting off the phone when he came home after work so I could pay attention to him, by not scheduling meetings at night with the women I sponsor, and by spending some time with him at parties talking to other couples instead of immediately heading for my girlfriends whom I'd just seen earlier that day at a meeting. I asked his opinion and honored his answers. I can think of more examples, but you get the idea. He was important in my life, and I made sure he knew it! The only "rule" was that my attention had to be genuine and truthful.

Just as I discovered that it's not possible to tear down *his* self-esteem without tearing down my own, I found that it's not possible to build *up* his self-esteem without building up mine as well.

We learned to work on ourselves rather than each other. It became more ingrained in each of us. We found that the more we changed, the more difficult it was for the other to continue their old behavior!

I was no longer responsible for how Bill felt. He was no longer responsible for how I felt. I couldn't blame him for my feelings ("you made me feel" is a lie!), and he couldn't blame me for his.

We found that almost all the problems in our relationship could be overcome by learning how to communicate effectively and honestly.

Our solution is a mutual dependence on a loving God as he may express himself in our group conscience. When this is central to our lives, we can achieve true partnership.

We began to grow up!

Life doesn't care what I like or don't like—it doesn't care a bit. My real purpose is to fit myself to be of maximum service to God and the people around me, right? But when I make myself the leader in the delusional world of *my* management, I become the reference point, not God. And when I do this, I cut myself off from the sunlight of the spirit, and I will wither and die.

I know everyone can take my stories of pain and spiritual growth and find examples of situations and solutions in their own lives and their own recovery process.

The essence of all growth is a willingness to change for the better and then an *unremitting* willingness to shoulder whatever responsibility this entails.

We had life and relationship problems *long* before we drank alcohol. Isn't it wonderful that we now have access to a Power and a program that removes the obsession to drink and helps us to learn how to become happy and usefully whole?

All we have to do is thoroughly follow the path.

Questions from Tradition Two

1. List seven attributes your higher power must have before you trust him to be your ultimate authority. (Examples: loving, forgiving, principled, sense of humor, etc.)

2. Who's the boss? How do I demonstrate that the God of my understanding is the real authority in my relationships?

3. Does one person dominate the other in my relationships? If yes, how is this manifested? If yes, what is the payoff for me? What do I get out of this arrangement?

4. *How do I participate as an equal in my relationships?*

5. *As an adult, am I discovering, examining, and discarding the destructive "old ideas" about relationships I observed as a child and believed to be "the truth"? Am I embracing the positive "old ideas"?*

6. *Do I believe my roles and rules are the only right ones?*

7. *In my relationships, how do I practice the principles of A.A. rather than the principles of my "old ideas?"*

8. *Do I have a working definition of "love" and share it with those I love? What is my definition?*

9. *What is the difference between humility and humiliation?*

10. *Do I always have to be right? Am I the A.A. "police?"*

11. *How do I try to "fix" other people? Do I "justifiably" criticize others?*

12. *Does "compromise" mean "to lose?" What is my definition of compromise? Am I willing to compromise?*

13. *Am I learning how to really listen to others, or am I thinking of my response while they are still talking?*

14. *How am I committed to learning and practicing healthy listening skills?*

15. *How am I committed to learning and practicing healthy communication skills?*

16. *How do I practice being a friend? How do I grow and maintain my relationships?*

17. *Do I talk openly and honestly about my feelings with my loved ones? If not, why not?*

18. *How do I try to practice the spirit of Saint Francis prayer in all my relationships?*

19. *Do I make unilateral decisions in my relationships, or do I first consult those involved?*

20. *How do I establish mutually agreeable, workable ground rules in my closest relationships?*

21. *How do I support the spiritual and emotional growth of my loved ones? Have I committed to resolving conflicts creatively? What does this look like?*

22. *Do I have any "gimmicks" to keep me God-conscious throughout the day? Apps on my phone, for example*

23. *Through my behavior, how do I support my loved ones' self-esteem?*

24. *How do I acknowledge the importance of others in my life?*

The Only Requirement!

Chapter Three

TRADITION THREE IN our book Twelve Steps and Twelve Traditions states that the only requirement for A.A. membership is a desire to stop drinking.

For our purposes, Tradition Three could be stated this way: The only requirement for a good personal relationship is a mutual desire to be in that relationship and a willingness to do the work necessary to have a healthy, reasonably happy relationship.

One person can't make a relationship work. Each person must be dedicated to the relationship and honor the concept of unity. Each must be willing to stay in the relationship and have a goal of growth in that relationship. This implies an atmosphere of acceptance of each other and each other's differences.

I had been married many times and had numerous failed friendships and acquaintances. What was the problem? My sponsor pointed out that I was the common denominator in all of them. I began to realize that as soon as the going got tough, I always ran. I ended relationships through divorce, avoidance, or by moving. Fight or flight? I chose *flight*. Geographical change was one of my primary coping skills. It always seemed like a good idea at the time, but as I look back on my life, I can see that no matter the relationship, it was never 100%. At most, it was 99%. I always had a loophole to avoid the pain of the work necessary to look at myself and make changes for our mutual benefit. "Compromise" was not in my vocabulary. My self-centeredness focused on the other person and made it their fault that the relationship wasn't working. My old attitude was, "You need to change so I'll feel better." I was defensive, arrogant, and always right. If you didn't cooperate and come around to my way of thinking, I severed the relationship without thought or regret, usually with a few choice words! I took my power back from you and moved on.

This was me until I came to Alcoholics Anonymous in 1975. I was told that drinking was just a symptom of what was wrong with me. I was told that once the symptom was removed, I had to learn how to live my life *differently* in order to stay away from the symptom. I had no idea what this meant. How could I live differently? My loving sponsor pointed out that "differently" meant "different attitude." My self-centered attitude must change for me to be truly sober. For me to change my attitude, I had to change my actions. "This is an action program," she said. A.A. stands for "*attitude adjustment*." This meant acting in a way that was different from my thoughts or feelings. My thoughts and feelings about everything were usually pretty negative. I thought this was normal. What to do, what to do? "Just bring the body, and the mind will follow," she said.

Because of difficult financial circumstances (I was broke), I lived with my father for the first seven months of my sobriety. On the second or third day after I had moved into his house, I found myself sinking into an old, comfortable thought pattern. I began to feel sorry for myself because other people had ruined my life. I was such a victim and a loser, and I would never be happy again. As I was thinking these spiraling thoughts and feeling these dismal feelings, the alcohol in my father's house began to call to me. You all know the usual pattern – my mind told me it would be different this time. I had had enough experience with this kind of thinking to realize I would drink, find momentary relief, and then be off in my addiction again. Tell me if you relate to *this:* before I came to A.A., I had such faith in alcohol that when I went *into* the liquor store, I felt better. I felt better just walking *out* of the store with my two bottles of scotch. I had yet to put a drink inside me, but the *thought* made me *feel* better! It shows you my problem centers in my mind rather than my body, doesn't it? I hadn't had anything to drink, but *I felt better.* By the way, I always bought two bottles and two cartons of cigarettes. I kept one set in my house and one set in my car. I figured my house wouldn't be robbed and my car stolen on the same day, so I'd always have access to at least one bottle of scotch and my cigarettes. I was so smart!

That is such crazy thinking!

It also shows how dependent I was on a power outside myself to do for me what I couldn't do for myself.

So, I was standing in my father's living room with these thoughts swirling around when suddenly, this voice came into my head: "What are you going to do about it **today?**" I was so startled that I answered the voice aloud, "Well, maybe I could get in my car during daylight and find the meeting I'm supposed to attend tonight. That way, when it's dark, I can't tell myself, "I don't know where the meeting is, and I don't want to get lost, so I won't go tonight; I'll find a meeting tomorrow."

Instead, I took action, found the meeting, and went that night. My actions and my behavior overcame my negative thoughts and feelings. The thought of drinking alcohol has not seriously entered my mind since that day.

I heard this at an early meeting: *I must act my way into good thinking; I can't think my way into good acting.* I didn't understand it but knew it was important, so I wrote it down. That sentence was to become the foundation of my sober life!

With my sponsor's insistence, I went to the women's meeting and tried to see what I could bring to the meeting rather than what I could get out of it. What a concept! It dawned on me that I could do this at every meeting. I began to consciously practice this attitude *outside* the rooms of A.A. and with the other people in my life. Wow!

My father and I had never gotten along. He was an alcoholic, and I had the "ism" even before I drank. Our wills clashed from the beginning of my life. Strangely enough, during those seven months, even though he continued to live his alcoholic life, I was sober and began to feel compassion for this man who had been a military hero in his younger days and now was just an old drunk, biding his time with alcohol until he died. I saw the sadness of the man, and I wanted to be helpful. What could I bring to our relationship to enhance it, not what could I get out of it? It was a beautiful and practical way to make amends. I could see the pain, bewilderment, and despair underneath the self-importance and bravado he showed me and the world.

Now, *that* is an attitude adjustment!

For the first time in my life, people became three-dimensional! My father, the people at the A.A. meetings, the clerk at the grocery store, the new woman at the meeting, the neighbor – *all became real like me!*

It sounds so simple as I rattle off this list, but let me tell you, it was one encounter at a time, one minute at a time. Each and every time, I had to make a *conscious decision* to be courteous no matter what.

I remember being snippy to a bank teller one day, walking out of the bank through the revolving door, and staying *in* that revolving door right back into the bank to apologize to that teller for my rude behavior. It's strange, but rather than feeling humiliated by having to say I was wrong, I felt great!

As my sponsor encouraged me to make friends with the women in the program, I tried to take the same other-centered approach. I was no longer completely consumed with my immature focus on "me, me, me."

"A state of self-absorption is in disharmony with the universal process so that, as with a dirty window, the light can't shine through." I read that somewhere.

I practiced caring about these women and their lives, asking *them* questions about *them* rather than going on and on about "me, me, me." Soon, I found that I really did care. I stopped comparing their outsides with my insides. I began to feel a part of. I began to feel that I belonged. My black-and-white world was becoming full of bright colors!

I began to value harmony and unity in my relationships. I became willing to make each relationship work amicably, no matter how brief. The funny thing is, I noticed that I was the one who felt good after a polite encounter and bad after a self-centered, arrogant one. This good feeling encouraged me to continue the practice of courtesy. My friend Don said, *"I have found I can't be discourteous and spiritual at the same time!"*

Through my actions, I became willing to make those 100% commitments I had avoided all my life. I became willing to go *through* the hard times (disagreements, differences of opinion, different agendas) with these women without running or moving.

Life was good!

Oh, the blessed order of things! I didn't know it, but I needed all the practice I could get of being willing to work on "safe" relationships. I didn't know I was about to meet the "man of my dreams." I met Bill! *This became a whole new ballgame!* I was two years, and he was five years sober when we met at an A.A. meeting and began to date. I was five years, and he was nine years sober when we married.

I've written in previous chapters about how we came into our marriage with lots of baggage and preconceived notions and the battles that occurred as a result of our mutual, self-centered fears. This baggage had been accumulating while each of us was growing up in our very dissimilar households. We had very different values and beliefs about marriage and the male/female relationship, especially the roles and rules for the man and the roles and rules for the woman. Bill was raised to be the absolute boss in the house; I was raised to be the absolute boss in the house, even though I had to boss by manipulation, not overtly. These roles were largely unconscious, unspoken, and *very real.* You can imagine the bewilderment and anger we both felt when we tried to practice our roles and rules on each other and were thwarted by the other just playing their role!

I know now that if we could have done better, we would have done better. Each of us had the burden of the bondage of self to overcome and a whole new set of life skills to learn. Even though I was sober, I was doing the same old things and getting the same old results!

It really was simple, although it seemed overwhelming. It turns out that the majority of our problems revolved around poor communication skills, male/female issues left over from childhood, and a lack of a sustainable spiritual orientation. We had to learn how to apply the principles of *humility* and *unity* to our personal lives, creating mutual respect and an openness to new perspectives.

We had the only requirement for membership in our group of two. Most of the time we desired to be in our relationship and were willing to do the work necessary to grow into a healthy relationship. *We just didn't know **how** to do this.* Our two sponsors taught us to value unity and to put God as the loving and *only* authority in our marriage. They taught us to put into **action** what we had learned in Alcoholics Anonymous. They also taught us techniques, skills we didn't possess, to navigate the marital relationship more lovingly.

We were taught to study and utilize "Fair Fighting." Fair Fighting is a way to manage conflict and its associated feelings effectively. It became the most important and effective tool in our new toolbox! Because we had never learned how to manage our anger *constructively*, we handled it inappropriately, never reaching an agreed-upon solution to *any* problem. Our group of two had different approaches to dealing with anger: we had the "mad bomber," who got angry quickly but with little control. At the other end of the spectrum, we had the "smolderer" who stored up complaints and didn't express them directly. Instead, this one acted out angry feelings in passive ways.

We were always going to have some disagreements, but the quality of our relationship showed up in how we *resolved* these disagreements. To Fight Fair, we learned to follow some basic guidelines to keep our disagreements from becoming destructive. This was difficult because I usually thought Bill's point of view was irrational, stupid, and unfair. Little did I know he was thinking the same thing about *my* ideas!

Here are some ground rules we learned and, more importantly, *practiced*:

Ground Rules for Fair Fighting:

REMAIN CALM.

We tried not to overreact to difficult situations. If I remained calm, it was more likely that Bill would consider my viewpoint. I tend to get excited and raise my voice. When I do that, it sounds like I'm angry and looking for a fight. Actually, in the days before A.A., I *was* angry and looking for a fight. Now, I was trying to learn a new and more effective way of conducting my life, no matter how wrong it initially felt. So I had to learn how to calm down and speak softly. This took a lot of effort on my part. It went against *everything* I wanted to do, everything I'd learned to do!

EXPRESS FEELINGS IN WORDS, NOT ACTIONS.

Telling someone directly and honestly how I feel can be a very powerful form of communication. If I get too angry or upset, wanting to shout or throw things, I call a 'time out' until I feel calmer. Sometimes, I take a brief walk; sometimes, I play with our dog – whatever works.

BE SPECIFIC ABOUT WHAT IS BOTHERING ME.

Vague complaints are hard to work with. "Your attitude makes me crazy!" is not a complaint that can easily be solved! What attitude? About what? And, by the way, his attitude is *his* business! Let's try for something more complaint-worthy, like "When you throw your dirty socks at the hamper, and they land on the floor beside the hamper, it bothers me that you don't pick them up and put them in the hamper. I feel that you think I'm your servant, that picking them up is beneath you, but not me. I feel disrespected." How's that for specific? That's what his father did, and his mother never complained. Bill didn't mean anything by it – nothing personal. We discussed it, and he began putting his dirty socks in the hamper. Not because I made him do it but because we were partners with a common goal of having a neat and tidy house, and he respected me. Since we had talked with each other openly and without *self-righteous* anger, we could arrive at a mutually agreed-upon solution. We learned that a successful relationship depends on how well we send and receive messages. It also depends on honesty in what we say and understanding what we hear.

DEAL WITH ONLY ONE ISSUE AT A TIME.

Don't introduce other topics until each is thoroughly discussed. This avoids the *"kitchen sink"* effect, where we throw in all our complaints without allowing anything to be resolved. "You *always* leave your dirty socks by the hamper, and you *never* turn out a light when you leave the room, and you *never* open a door for me like Suzie's husband does, and, by the way, you were rude to my father the other day." Now there's a kitchen sink full of complaints!

NO "HITTING BELOW THE BELT."

Attacking areas of personal sensitivity creates an atmosphere of distrust, anger, and vulnerability. Disparaging the qualities of his beloved yet deceased father is hitting below the belt. Talking about his need to wear glasses as if it were a character defect he could ask God to remove is hitting below the belt.

AVOID ACCUSATIONS.

This will cause the other to react defensively, to defend themselves. Instead, we were to talk about how we *felt*. This is where that "you made me feel" thing comes in.

Accusing him of something he is incapable of doing is a foolish accusation. It took me a really long time to accept that no one can *make* me feel anything. How I feel is my choice. My *perceptions* usually dictate how I feel. Here's an example: I can define a glass as half full or half empty. It's all about my attitude! How I define something determines how I feel, not some guy saying something I can interpret a million different ways – it's my choice.

DON'T GENERALIZE.

Avoid words like "you never" and "you always." Such generalizations are usually inaccurate and will heighten tensions. "You never listen to me!" isn't true. Obviously, he must listen to me some of the time. Otherwise, how would he know he has a choice of either broccoli or cauliflower for dinner or "I've made reservations at your favorite restaurant" unless he listened? When I generalize, it's easy to have the conversation deteriorate down to him defensively reciting a list of times he claims he *did* listen, and the communication gets way off track!

AVOID "MAKE BELIEVE."

Exaggerating or inventing a complaint – or your feelings about it – will prevent real issues from surfacing. Stick with the facts and your honest feelings. This goes back to the "you always " and "you never " kind of communication. It's a dead-end street. I can't do much in the way of resolution with something so vague and untrue.

DON'T STOCKPILE.

Storing up lots of grievances and hurt feelings over time is *so* counterproductive. It's almost impossible to deal with numerous old problems for which *interpretations* may differ. Try to deal with issues as they arise. I was really good at "stockpiling." I could create a list of grievances that went back 20 years. It was kind of like piling up ammunition. When the war came, I was ready! And I never forgot even one of those grievances!

AVOID "CLAMMING UP."

Positive results can only be attained with *two-way* communication. When one person becomes silent and stops responding to the other, frustration and anger can result. Bill was really good at this form of non-communication. He would simply walk away from a "discussion," leaving me ready to tear my hair out because I still had things to say. I remember one time I followed him out the front door, still talking. He got in his car and drove away, and I was still talking! I say "talking" – I was shouting at the retreating vehicle! I think that's why our sponsors had us sit knee to knee, holding hands when we wanted to discuss *anything*. The kind of **silent avoidance** Bill used became a control issue. Sitting still and holding hands meant neither of us could easily get up and walk away. This is different from taking a legitimate "time-out."

ESTABLISH COMMON GROUND RULES.

Read and discuss these ground rules. Insert some of your own. This mutually agreed-upon understanding will go a long way in managing and resolving conflict. When we had our list of ground rules, we checked them with our sponsors and printed them out. In the beginning, we each held our own little copy in our hands, ready to pounce if the other deviated from the rules! Soon, we knew the rules and no longer needed the printed page.

Fair Fighting – Step by Step:

Before you begin, ask yourself, "What exactly is bothering me?" "What do I want the other person to do or not do?" "Are my feelings in proportion to my issue?" In other words, was I overreacting? (See the rule 'remain calm' for the answer to that.)

Know what your goals are before you begin. What are the possible outcomes that would be acceptable to you? Of course, my goal usually was to get my way. I had to rethink this "goal" thing to include our *mutual goals*. This was a foreign concept to me. I always had *my* goal and expected you to hop on the bandwagon because it obviously was the right thing to do.

Remember that our goal is not to "win" but to come to a mutually satisfying and peaceful solution to the problem. As a fighter, this was a difficult concept for me to grasp. My mentality said if I didn't "win," I "lost." That had been my attitude my whole life. There was no middle ground, no compromise in my vocabulary. It was hard for me to see that if I "won" the battle, I "lost" the war. I had to redefine the word "win." The funny thing is, when I successfully controlled my thoughts and emotions, and we came to an agreeable solution, I felt great! I felt a true sense of *partnership*. I felt a closer kinship with Bill. We were in this thing together!

Set a time for a discussion with your partner-in-conflict. It should be as soon as possible, but agreeable to both persons. Springing something when the other is unprepared may leave the other person feeling that they must fend off an attack. If you encounter resistance to setting a time, try to help the other person see that the problem is important to you. In the beginning, Bill and I set aside time every evening to sit knee to knee – you know the rest of the drill. We each had a printout of the "Fair Fighting" rules and would refer to them as we talked, especially if we felt the other was violating one of the rules.

State the problem clearly. Our ability to communicate effectively was almost non-existent – we had never learned how to talk so the other would listen or how to listen so the other would talk. We weren't aware that we had our own rules and roles for communicating and that they were different. We learned that neither of us was right or wrong; we just had different *communication styles*. My mother taught me it was "peace at any price," but get your way by manipulating the truth. Bill learned from his father that he would get his way if he were a bully. These attitudes showed up when we would try to discuss a "problem," No wonder we needed our sponsors to be referees! *We were just playing a role; there was no authenticity to either one of us.* We had to learn how to truly accept each other as real people, not just barriers to getting our own way. Through the dreaded exercise we had to do each evening, we learned that true acceptance of the other, warts and all, encouraged both of us to feel safe – safe enough to be open to a genuine and loving relationship.

We learned that it wasn't **what** we said to each other but **how** we said it that was important.

We all know people that we feel talk down to us as if they are smart and we are stupid. They seem so condescending. We tend to avoid them, or at least to avoid being our vulnerable selves with them, because we feel anything we say or do could become potential ammunition they could use against us. These people usually feel pretty isolated, so they double down on their efforts to get close to us, and we move further away. You can see the pattern here. What if we discovered that their *apparent* attitude was simply their tone of voice, a way of talking they learned as a child from their mother? What if they were totally unaware of the silent message of contempt they were conveying? What if they learned the technique of modulating their voice so they were just one individual talking to an equal? How would you feel about them then? What kind of relationship would it be possible to have? If I was the culprit, I was almost always unaware of the unspoken message I was sending. I was paying attention to the *words*, not my tone of voice! It wasn't my intent to be disrespectful; it was my technique that carried that message. Silent messages are conveyed through our behavior as well. I had to learn how to change my *behavior* to one of consideration and love. I had no idea when we first got married that Bill would feel unimportant if I disappeared after dinner to spend the evening with a woman I sponsored. Since neither she nor I worked, we could have gotten together any time during the day while Bill was at work. Once I understood the situation from *Bill's* point of view, I changed my plans with these women, and we met during the day.

One of the best tools I ever learned was walking *from the prosecution table around to the defense table.* This alters how I *define* something. Instead of feeling angry that Bill was interfering with my program, I felt terrible that he felt so unimportant as a result of the unspoken message I was giving him. I began to try to see the problem through my partner's point of view. The "opposing" viewpoint can make sense even if I disagree.

Invite your partner-in-conflict to share their point of view while you use active listening skills. Be careful not to interrupt, and genuinely listen to their concerns and feelings. It might be helpful to restate what you've heard in a way that lets your partner know you have fully understood. Ask your partner to do the same for you.

At first, try to stick to the facts; then, once you've stated the facts, state your feelings. Use "I" messages to describe your feelings of anger, hurt, or disappointment. Avoid "You" messages like, "You make me angry." In the beginning, we really needed our sponsors' help to state the problem clearly. We usually didn't know exactly what the problem was, just that we were unhappy and that it was the other person's fault. Sponsors helped us get down to the real issues. Several times, our sponsors suggested professional help (See page 133 in our book Alcoholics Anonymous.). Together and separately, we resolved some deep-seated issues that interfered with a healthy relationship.

Most of the time, our problems originate from feeling disrespected. This could take the form of not being listened to, not being consulted in something involving both of us, feeling controlled by the other, and feeling manipulated. These were all *feelings*, of course, and even though feelings aren't facts, feelings are valid. **Feelings aren't facts, but**

feelings are valid. Once we could identify the problem, the solution became almost obvious. My sponsor taught me this trick of *active listening* : as the other person speaks, I silently repeat the words they are saying to myself. This stops me from forming my response while they are talking and means that I'll truly understand what they have said when they stop talking. Only then can I respond based on what they've said, not on what I've halfway heard. By the way, *this is hard work!*

Propose specific solutions and invite the other person to propose solutions. For example, the problem can be stated as: "When you meet with the women you sponsor during the only time we have together, I feel that you don't care about me or respect me." If I'd listened to him without getting defensive and lashing out, the healthy solution to our communication problem could have been resolved by coming up with a mutually agreed-upon compromise. When I changed the time of my meeting with the women I sponsored, the message I was conveying to Bill, and the message he was receiving was the *same*: "I respect and love you enough to want to spend time with you."

Discuss the advantages and disadvantages of each pro-posal. This required honesty, willingness, and an open mind. I didn't have too much trouble with honesty and willingness; it was the open mind that I had the most difficulty with. I was always right! Well, maybe not always. Then I would be reminded that I had promised to go to any lengths to achieve a healthy, harmonious relationship. My closed mind began to open to the slight possibility that Bill might have a good idea after all.

Be ready for some compromise. Allowing the other person only one course of action will likely hinder resolution (now **there's** an understatement!). When there is agreement on a proposal for change, celebrate! Even if it's *his* proposal? Yes, even if it's his proposal!

Set a trial period for the new behavior. At the end of the trial period, you can discuss the possibility of modifying or continuing the change. If no solution has been reached regarding the original problem, schedule a time to begin the discussion again. We didn't have a problem with this one, because the sanity of the new, healthy behavior became apparent to both of us, and tension in the home and in our relationship lessened.

Sometimes, despite our best fair-fighting efforts, a disagreement or conflict seemed insurmountable. This occurred twice during our early marriage. With our sponsors' blessings, we consulted a trained professional. She helped us communicate more effectively, and we worked our way towards solutions.

Bill and I resolved most of our conflicts using our loving higher powers, our sponsors, and the Twelve Steps and Twelve Traditions. The more we used these tools to work things out, the easier and more natural it became. Repetition, repetition, repetition is the only way to change old habits and old ideas!

I had to learn that conflict is a normal, inevitable, and even healthy aspect of most relationships. I thought a perfect relationship meant always agreeing on everything. When managed well, disagreements can strengthen relationships with friends, family members, co-workers, and romantic partners. **Fair Fighting** provides many tools and techniques to help us achieve positive results when problems arise.

Occasionally, one of us would be *momentarily* unwilling to make the effort. Thank God, usually, the other would take up the slack and be kind and loving enough to carry us through. On the days when we *both* were in our baby high chairs demanding immediate gratification we both had a bad day!

It's funny how, in those days, I could go to an A.A. meeting and be loving, wise, and tolerant, then go home and be a screaming, self-centered madwoman! In my head, I knew my real purpose was to fit myself to be of maximum service to God and the people around me. But surely this didn't apply to me *at home!* With *that* rotten person?

There were times when I told myself, "I'm going to work real hard on *me* and become perfect. Then I'll leave this idiot for a man who deserves me!"

Oops! Back to the 99% commitment!

Fortunately, we both usually didn't feel the same way on the same day, and gradually, I began to see the absurdity and the insanity in my attitude. We adopted **Rule 62**: we stopped taking ourselves so seriously. We even learned to laugh at some of our old ideas about relationships. By the way, Rule 62 is explained in detail in the Fourth Tradition.

We'll be talking more about this wonderful attitude adjustment tool in future chapters.

Bill and I began to let go of our old ideas and form new ones that *we* chose – as partners, not adversaries. My friend Sandy told her boyfriend when he proposed to her, "I will marry you one day at a time." What a great idea! Each day, I will make that 100% commitment to healthy relationships with other human beings. Each day, when I get on my knees to ask God to keep me away from a drink of alcohol today, I will also ask God to keep me in loving and courteous relationships for this day, even with my husband!

Amazing things happen when I ask God for help with a problem I don't have the power to solve. Just as I don't have the power *not* to drink alcohol, I don't have the power to change me.

The Big Book says the origin and engine of my alcoholism is self-centeredness. I cannot effectively treat it with any form of self-obsession, even if I dress up my perception of self in spiritual clothing!

With the pain of continuous collisions of wills in my life, I began to be willing to change my behavior whether I felt like it or not, whether I approved or not.

Transformation (change without any effort on my part) is addictive, progressive, and cumulative. Just as when I was drinking alcohol, the better I felt, the more I wanted to feel better, and the more willing I was to take the *actions* necessary to bring about that feeling.

I felt better when my attitude changed from self-centered defensiveness to unity and love. I began to crave that feeling of ease and comfort that came about from acting like a grown-up!

In A.A., I "discovered" a power I call God, who had always been there, although I didn't know it. He believed in me even when I didn't believe in him. I began to see the love and help he was giving me and had *always* given me. I saw that only my faulty self-reliance blocked God's always generous gifts.

I began to ask for help to improve my relationships. I stopped giving God a list of my demands. Somehow, that seemed counterproductive for a Power greater than myself. That was a more appropriate list for Santa Claus!

I still seek to improve my conscious contact with this Power on a daily basis. To acknowledge the nature of my relationship with God, I get on my knees each morning and night and turn my life and will over to his care. When I ask for his guidance and try to follow it, I find that he manages my life better than I ever did. He comes up with goodies I could never even imagine! Usually, I can't see how anything good can come out of my current problems. I can't see God's big picture. This is where persistence and faith come in. Over the years, I have learned that *my* job is to adjust my attitude and be willing to seek and do God's will in the present – in the now – and leave the future to God.

All I have to do to reinforce this idea is to look back at the situation I was in when I got sober. I couldn't drink, couldn't not drink, was broke, had to live with my father, couldn't date, and had to behave in strange and very uncomfortable ways with my sponsor and other women – how was this ever going to have a good outcome? I now believe I was in enough pain that I was willing to accept directions from a sober woman and take some actions that

I felt were all wrong! Thus was born a shaky faith which has grown and grown over the years because I continue to do the next right thing right, despite my doubts and self-centered fears!

Each day, I have a choice: I can live in my old ideas of a hostile world or I can look at the world as I believe God does, through the eyes of love and tolerance of others. When I define my attitude as my **behavior** rather than my **thinking** or **feeling**, it becomes easier to maintain that attitude. My behavior toward Bill changed from enemy to partner because we had a 100% commitment to that relationship, and God had become our only loving Authority. I was able to react to Bill with thoughts and feelings of love and compassion. This attitude carried over into my relations with other people as well. I began to find unity and harmony in my relationship with God when I remembered he is the father, and I am only one of his very special children among every other special children! Because of the awesome results of this attitude, I began to *want* to seek and do his will.

The actions I take on a minute-to-minute basis determine the *quality* of my sobriety and the *quality* of my life.

When I take the actions of a spiritually fit woman, I begin to change. Sometimes, I wonder how I could ever have believed so fervently in the "rightness" of my old ideas.

I have had a profound alteration in my reaction to life. Of course, *today,* I have no idea what old ideas I still harbor just under the surface of my awareness or what new ideas are beginning to form. Only time, life, and a loving God will reveal more of me to me!

I don't regret any of my sober experiences, just as I don't regret any of my experiences throughout my life – before drinking, during drinking, and in sobriety. If I erased all the mistakes of my past, I would also erase all the wisdom of my present. I needed every one of those experiences to become the person I am today. I earned my seat in Alcoholics Anonymous!

I have written about many ways I learned and *am* learning the desirability of a universal membership that includes me, God, and the people around me. All that is required is the rudimentary principle of honesty, the yearning to belong, an open mind, and the willingness to take specific actions. We are blessed to have the directions offered in the Twelve Steps and Twelve Traditions. All we have to do is manifest them in our daily lives, and the miracle will occur.

Guaranteed.

Questions from Tradition Three

1. *How do my actions show that I am 100% committed to my close personal relationships? Give examples.*

2. *How do I ask a God of my understanding to keep me in a loving and courteous attitude one day at a time?*

3. *How am I willing to do the work necessary to have healthy relationships? Give examples.*

4. *What exactly do I mean by "work"? Does it involve me working on myself and not the other person?*

5. *Do I concentrate on what I can bring to a relationship rather than what I can get from it?*

6. *Do I know how to communicate, or do I just talk? Give examples.*

7. *Am I able to share my feelings? Am I able to listen with an open mind to the feelings of another?*

8. *Am I willing to compromise? What does this mean to me?*

9. *Am I willing to go through the regular hard times in a relationship (unexpected life situations, differences of opinions, disagreements, different ways of doing things) without immediately terminating the relationship and blaming the other for its failure?*

Fair Fighting Questions for the Individual

1. *Am I able to remain calm?*

2. *Do I express my feelings in actions, not just words?*

3. *Am I specific about what is bothering me?*

4. *Do I deal with only one issue at a time?*

5. *Do I "hit below the belt"?*

6. *Do I avoid accusations: "You make me feel..."?*

7. *Do I generalize: "You always..." or "You never..."?*

8. *Do I exaggerate or invent a complaint?*

9. *Do I "stockpile"? Do I store up grievances?*

10. *Do I "clam up"? Practice the "silent treatment?"*

Fair Fighting Instructions

Print out the questions listed above for the individual.

- Give a copy to each person.
- Establish your mutual goals as a couple.
- Set a specific time for your discussion.
- State the problem clearly.
- Each person shares their point of view.
- Use active listening skills.
- Propose specific solutions
- Discuss the pros and cons of each proposal.
- Be willing to compromise.
- Set a trial period to practice new behavior.
- Be willing to consult a trained professional if necessary.
- Above all, show *respect* for others in your words, tone of voice, and actions! You want others to treat you that way, don't you?

Autonomy Matters!

"**EACH GROUP IS** autonomous except in matters affecting other groups or A.A. as a whole."

For our purposes, the Fourth Tradition could read: "Each person should be autonomous in the relationship except in matters affecting each other, the relationship itself, or others in our lives."

I have already written about the fact that unity is the underlying theme of *all* the traditions. Each tradition explains one specific way to protect the **unity** of the fellowship and the group, which also applies to the **unity of individual relationships**.

One person can't make a relationship work – *each* person must be dedicated to the relationship and honor the concept of "unity." Each must have a willingness to stay *in* the relationship and have a goal of growth in that relationship.

In other words, the individuals involved should not be overly dependent spiritually, mentally, or emotionally in the marriage or any relationship, lest ego inflation or deflation problems divert us from happy and healthy relationships of equals.

I looked up "autonomous," which means "self-governing." It means "not subject to control from outside. Independent. Existing and functioning as an independent organism."

This is a challenge all by itself. This is what the Twelve Steps are all about – the *spiritual awakening to who and what I am.* I am a product of a higher power. I am one of God's kids. I am me. There is only one me. When Dr. Bob's sidekick at the hospital, Sister Ignatia, was asked to speak at one of the first A.A. Conferences, she started her talk this way: she looked out at the audience and said: *"There's no one Youier than you!"* How profound is that?

Through the Twelve Steps, I discovered that the way to absolute freedom is in my association with a power greater than myself and my desire to seek and do that power's will in my life – *even in my relationships*. This is where the guidance of the Traditions comes in.

No one person can supply all the needs of another. We are each responsible for taking care of ourselves and for having a *balance* in our relationships. Our separateness is our mutual strength, promoting a partnership of healthy equals.

The poet Kahlil Gibran says it best:

On Marriage:

Let there be spaces in your togetherness
And let the winds of heaven dance between you
Sing and dance together and be joyous, but let
each one of you be alone.
And stand together but not too near together
*For the pillars of the temple stand apart, and the
oak tree and the cypress grow not in each other's
shadow.*

It has been my hard-earned, hard-learned experience that each partner should support the other spiritually, emotionally, and physically, but in a *balanced* fashion. In a *responsible* fashion. A grown-up person doesn't neurotically do for another grown-up person what they can do for themselves.

Here's what I mean. I have always exhibited what I call the "*merge urge.*" Even as a little kid, I would meet someone, attach myself to them like a *barnacle*, adopt their way of thinking and believing, and depend on them to take care of my needs in return for my undying loyalty.

Undying until it wasn't. This applied to everyone in my life. When I was done, I'd turn my back on the relationship and run, with absolutely no thought for the feelings of others – unless they ran first.

This kind of thinking was only possible because I was 100% self-centered! I could only see others as a means of satisfying *my* needs and wants. As long as other people are only actors on *my* stage, as long as they are only there to speak *my* lines and play the role *I* have assigned them, it's easy, as the ***director*** in everyone's life, to dump them when they are no longer useful.

How arrogant and grandiose is that? And yet, underneath that surface arrogance was a great dependency. I *depended* on these "actors" to play their roles and to read *my* lines. This would make *me* happy. This would make ***them*** happy. I had been taught that happiness was ***outside of me***, in people, places, and things. I suffered from an unconscious, ever-present *anxiety,* knowing that I had no real power to control those actors. In reality, *they* had the power, and I gave it to them!

The other person in my life became my 99% God for the moment. My partner or friend became my crutch in life. I needed them to play their role so I could play mine! This is a *faulty dependency*.

In A.A., I learned that there was a better way of living than emotionally depending on another human being for my sense of well-being. It was only when I recognized that I was sick and tired of being sick and tired that I became willing to challenge my whole belief system: my beliefs about love, happiness, and the right and wrong way to do things.

In A.A., I learned that I had been programmed – *I programmed myself!* "**Some of us tried to hold onto our old ideas.**" I really didn't want to look at my belief system because if I did, I might have to *change*. I might learn something *new*. My first reaction to anything new was *fear*. I read somewhere that this fear was not of the *unknown*. I really feared the loss of the *known* – the comfortable, safe, familiar *known*.

I always *appeared* to accept the role of follower in my relationships. It never occurred to me to take a leadership role in my own life and end up where *I* wanted to be rather than where someone was taking me. I accepted the value system that said *other people's opinions of me were more important than **my** opinion of me*. This is one of those old ideas that goes way back to childhood. I was a mixed bag of my parental programming, my experiences, my judgments, **and** my self-programming. I used to think that pain was in letting go of these old ideas, but I discovered it's not the *letting go*; it's the *holding on* that's painful. It's the **resistance to change**, the clinging to the familiar, that's painful. The more I resist something, the more power I give it. To the extent that I give people (past or present, living or dead) power over my feelings and my life, it's power *I* have given them. I learned in A.A. that I can take that power back at any time.

While I was overly dependent, I was at the same time a control freak in a very passive-aggressive way.

Two sides of the same coin.

The other side of that coin is the control aspect of the **need to be needed**, my dependence on others for my legitimacy. This is such an indication of low self-esteem. My importance was *validated* by being needed. I had an over-developed sense of responsibility to help others. I played God. I became a care*taker* rather than a care*giver*.

You may be shaking your head and saying, "What does all this have to do with Tradition Four?" It has *everything* to do with Tradition Four because I am describing *why*

I desperately needed Tradition Four. I'm describing the thinking and belief system I brought to Alcoholics Anonymous. *Tradition Four is all about emotional sobriety.* Bill Wilson calls emotional sobriety "The Next Frontier."

I don't need the Steps and Traditions as a "self-help" exercise. I need the Steps and Traditions because the person I brought to A.A. was incapable of having a healthy relationship with another human being. My *thinking* was so unhealthy I couldn't grasp the concept that "love and tolerance of others is our code." I needed to be *transformed*, but for that to happen, I needed to be able to see the unhealthy reality of my thinking. My sponsor was right when she told me, as a newcomer, "Rena, you are so sick you would only attract a sick man. Your drinking was only a symptom of your spiritual malady. Make yourself into a healthy woman, and you will attract a healthy man." She convinced me not to date the first year – I agreed with her. By the time I got to A.A., I knew there was more wrong with me than just drinking. What do *you* think my chances of forming a good and healthy relationship were at this point?

Ok, back to unraveling Tradition Four.

With my obsessive, unhealthy need to be needed, there was no way I could be autonomous. The most powerful lessons I learned about my dependency I learned through *sponsorship – me being the sponsor.* I began sponsoring when I was a year sober. I had no idea how much I needed to be needed by the women I sponsored. I felt that to be essential to their well-being, I had to be in charge, give advice on all their life issues, and then make sure they followed this advice. If they didn't, I tried harder to convince them I was right. I was a helper, a "fixer," and an enabler. I was creating *sick dependencies* in those I was trying to help.

When they did follow my advice, I felt warm and fuzzy with the security of knowing I was being "helpful." I felt good because I was needed. I could visualize them standing up to get their yearly medallion, thanking me for *saving their life* and *owing their sobriety to me, me, me!* It took me a while to realize I placed my self-esteem in the hands of others, and if they rejected me or left me, I felt worthless. I had no idea how dependent I was on the opinions of other people to make me feel OK.

I was seven years sober when I was "fired" by a woman I had sponsored since she was a newcomer in A.A. We were so close that she had become a part of my family; we did everything together, and I was the acknowledged boss of her life. One day, she told me she had to get another sponsor because we were so close she couldn't talk to me. *I was devastated!* What would people think? How could I explain this to the other women I sponsored? I wanted to run, hide, move away, and start over. **I wanted to get away from the way I felt**! I called my sponsor, weeping and wailing. "Good for her," she said. "She's taking care of her sobriety." *What?*

Slowly, and with my sponsor Tommie's help, I began to see that my faulty dependencies victimized me. I began to see the underlying ego-feeding reasons for my need to control. I began to see that *sponsorship is not ownership.* I started to learn to be a good and effective sponsor by *detaching emotionally* from their problems and from "fixing" them. I stopped trying to save them from the pain of spiritual growth. I supported their *sobriety.* The only "advice" I gave came straight out of the Big Book or the Twelve and Twelve. I shared my experience, strength, and hope, but only as sober encouragement, not as hard and fast rules. *I stopped taking responsibility for their lives in an effort to prove my worthiness!*

From this new viewpoint, I had another "AHA" moment where I began to examine my problems with *other* relationships – my friendships, my grown child, my co-workers – all of my relationships. I started to ask God to help me let go of my unhealthy dependence on these relationships as well. After all, it was about **me**, not them! This was good news: since the problem was in me, I didn't have to wait for them to change so I'd feel better. I also began to see the bigger picture. I started to **want** to be more emotionally and spiritually independent. The best part of being free from these dependencies and open to others is that I no longer have to pretend. I don't have to pretend I have all the answers. I don't have to lie and then remember what I said. It cuts way back on the anxiety I had lived with all my life because I was living a lie and was afraid of being exposed.

And yet, I had been entirely unaware of all of this.

I live my life forward but understand it backward. When I look back, I see how skewed my thinking was: my life was really taking place between my ears, in my addictive thinking. I always *thought* I would be happy if I had a new man or a new dress. I *thought* I would be happy when I cut my hair or moved to a new city. I was always looking outside of myself for peace and contentment. It wasn't just people I made my higher power. Throughout my life, I also made *money* a kind of underlying higher power. I *thought* I would be happy if I only had the money to buy...(fill in the blank.)

Oh, and I almost forgot – I was so self-centered that I thought *I* was my higher power! *(You know the difference between me and God? He never thinks he's me!)*

Here's the weird part: even with these grandiose ideas about myself, I still felt like I had no power and was a victim of other people's power.

You have been getting a good idea of who I was when I entered Alcoholics Anonymous and my transformation began. By the way, transformation always involves the peeling away of everything we have relied upon, leaving us feeling the world as we know it is coming to an end – and it is.

Of course, most of the suggestions I got when I came to you were not to my liking. "You drank every day; you can go to a meeting every day – get on your knees and ask *something* to keep you sober – it doesn't matter if you don't believe it – believe that I believe it!" Here's the biggie – I took the advice of my sponsor and agreed not to date that first year of my sobriety. Much later, I could see it was the greatest gift I ever gave myself. That year, I learned a little bit about who I was through meetings, working the Steps with my sponsor, and practicing life in an environment where I felt *safe*. I found that women made great friends; they were not just stupid or competitive, as I had always believed.

By the time I met Bill, I was slightly more sane than when I first got sober. I was still self-centered. Everything, including my friendships with women, revolved around me, me, me. I had completed my year – and more – of *not dating* when I met the "man of my dreams." I was two years sober, and Bill was five. It was the instant meshing of neuroses! My education about relationships was suddenly ramped up into high gear! I still didn't know how to have a healthy relationship *with a man*. You will note that I defined any relationship *with a man* as a category separate and different from a relationship with anyone else!

It started innocently enough. We dated for three years before we married. *It was wonderful. **Bill*** was wonderful. *I* was wonderful.

When we disagreed, we never argued. We would separate, go to our respective homes, nurse our grudges, and then get back together as if nothing had happened. We never discussed whatever it was that had caused the disagreement. When we were growing up, this is how we had each seen our parents handle conflict – by ignoring it. Now, maybe they resolved issues when we weren't around, but we didn't know that part. We had each assumed that pretending it wasn't there was the *right* way, the *grown-up way,* to deal with unpleasantness. *We did love that elephant in the living room!* We dated for three years and bragged we had the perfect relationship because we never argued!

And then we married and lived in the same house!

Now, the *rules and roles* began to change. Now, we were fighting for control. Is it any wonder we suddenly had relationship problems? Bill and I were both operating from a base of self and self-protection. Instead of acting as **equal partners** in an autonomous group of two, we were adversaries, not partners, each clinging to the idea that our way was right and that the other had to change to make the relationship work.

When I look back at those days, I must remember that we were completely unaware of these negative, fear-driven attitudes. We were simply *reacting* to life the way we had learned as children. When we were afraid we would lose something we had or not get something we wanted, we lashed out in childish anger. The result was always the same. We were two children in adult bodies, and we felt hurt, frustrated, and confused most of the time. *It wasn't fair. It wasn't supposed to be this way. And it was all your fault!*

Some days, I felt, "If I don't get away from him *right now,* I will die!" "Why can't Bill see the obvious truth," I would cry to my sponsor, "*He's wrong* !" This was the point in time where I usually dumped a relationship and moved on, full of self-pity and righteous anger, because **once again**, someone had failed me.

It wasn't until one day when I said to my sponsor, in pain and desperation, "Maybe I'm a **little bit** at fault in this mess," that she said, "Great! Now **you don't have to leave or wait around for *him* to change so *you'll* feel better!** Now, *what do **you** want to do about it?*"

She always put all the responsibility for my happiness right back on *me.* I had no idea that I automatically blamed others for *everything*, even my drinking. I don't know where or when I learned to shift responsibility from me to you, but it was so ingrained it was largely unconscious. It also made me a victim of everyone and everything on the planet!

The *good* news is that if I acted *autonomously and self-governed and took responsibility for my life and my choices, I would no longer be* under the control of everybody and everything.

The *bad* news is that if I took responsibility for my life and my choices, I couldn't *blame* everybody and everything – it was no longer possible for me to be a victim. I was now officially a volunteer.

This was another *tiny* release from **the bondage of self**, although it seemed to me to be just another ego deflation at depth!

Through the loving guidance of our sponsors, our respective higher powers, and our determination to stick it out (stubbornness has its good points sometimes!), Bill and I launched ourselves *and* our marriage on a course of action that changed the way we thought and felt. We found we had to become aware of, examine, and let go of most of our old ideas. We learned that we had to emphasize achieving and maintaining emotional sobriety and peace of mind. For this, we *both* needed to practice our Twelve-Step spiritual programs. We also needed to develop much-needed skills to deal with our emotions and communicate effectively. By the way, no communication skill is more important than learning to communicate assertively. Assertively does *not* mean aggressively or passively! In *assertive communication*, I learn to express my *feelings* (**not my opinions**) in a manner in which no one gets hurt. Saying, "I feel....." expresses an honest emotion. Saying, "I feel *that*...." expresses an *opinion*. Think about it. Bill and I were often called upon to defend our opinions; we never had to defend our feelings.

I wrote extensively about ground rules and ways to Fight Fair in Tradition Three. I also wrote about our *personal conversational styles*. As children, we learn these individual styles by watching our parents or caregivers communicate. Sometimes, the **message** was completely different than their words, although *we* didn't see this. I wrote about people I've known whose conversational style made it *appear* to the listener that they were angry or talking down to others with contempt.

I wrote about the problems this caused in relationships. By learning to communicate effectively, this particular problem went away. It's funny how we usually only pay attention to the *words* we say, not the tone of voice we use to convey them. I still remember my mother saying nice things to me in a voice dripping with disapproval.

Now let's talk about the difference between *reacting* and *responding* and the enormous effect this has in communicating: here are some of the ways I have used to *react*:

- I completely forget my 12-Step program.
- I insist you are making me feel this way.
- I develop a long list of "shoulds" ("you should"...).
- I insist on fighting aggressively or passively
- I pout. I was really good at pouting.
- I don't tell him what's wrong. If he loved me, he would know.
- I get angry. I take it out on the dog, etc.
- I run away. Sleep on the couch. Clam up.
- I become a martyr. I become a victim.

Here are some other *negative coping skills* I have used in communicating:

- I justify my position. This leads to some interesting arguments as we *both* justify our positions;

- I get defensive. I know I am right, and explain this over and over again;

- I interrupt and talk over my partner. This makes the conversation deteriorate rapidly as we now are talking about the *other person* interrupting *all the time* instead of talking about our original issue;

- I become a mind reader. I insist I know what my partner *really* means even though he insists this wasn't what he meant at all;

- I complain back at him. If he complains about something I did or said, I bring up something and complain about *him*. This can really get us off track;

- I "kitchen sink" him. I wrote about this in the last chapter: I throw in everything he's ever done to annoy or defeat me. This makes it impossible to think or talk about one issue at a time;

- I make "winning" the goal. He has to lose so I can win, no matter what the cost to our relationship.

By the way, these negative "coping skills" can be used in dealing with **any** relationship, not just partners. No matter how casual or fleeting the relationship is, I can use these negative communication techniques on *anyone* to get my way and be perfectly perfect at the same time.

Before I talk about responding, I want to talk about *responding with empathy*. I looked it up. *Empathy* is the ability to say to oneself, "If I were this person in the same situation, I would feel just like he does."

With empathy, we can meet people where *they* are and not be angry because they aren't where *we* are.

Here are some ways I learned to *respond with empathy*:

- **Validation.** This means I can tell my partner, "I understand how you feel even though I disagree with your opinion." This says, "I understand your feelings and your right to have them, even though I don't share them." This is a beautiful way to show respect.

- **Active listening.** Probably the best and most important technique for real communication there is. I listen carefully and attentively to what the other person is saying, and then I can respond by saying, "What I heard you say was..." When I first began to use this skill, I was amazed at how often what I heard was not at all what the other person meant!

In the last chapter I wrote about a technique my sponsor taught me: as the other person speaks, I repeat their words silently to myself. This prevents me from forming my rebuttal *while they are talking*. It also clarifies in my head what they are actually saying. This is really hard work, by the way.

In difficult times, Bill and I learned first to *assume* we had a communication problem – that we just weren't communicating effectively with each other. It is *so* much easier to arrive at a solution *when we properly define the problem*. Otherwise, we are just sticking with the problem and blaming others for it!

One thing I must say that was of paramount importance to both of us: no matter what the problem, **Bill and I needed to keep our recovery programs and our meeting schedules intact.** *We couldn't spend so much time on our "problems" that we neglected the very thing that was helping us* **solve** *those problems.* If we backed away from our recovery programs, then we would have *two* problems: the relationship problem *and* the dry-drunk syndrome problem, which develops when an alcoholic doesn't treat his alcohol**ism.**

The Big Book states: "We have ceased fighting anyone or anything." We have entered the world of the spirit by establishing and practicing our *emotional independence.* This concept is really exciting!

We accomplish this when we don't allow other people to control our emotions. I've learned that others have only as much control over me as I give them. By remaining **emotionally autonomous**, I maintain power over my emotional state. I remember an old saying from the 60s – "What if they gave a war and nobody came?" This is true in personal relationships as well. It takes *two* to fight. I learned to ask myself, "How important is it?" "Is it worth getting upset about?" "Is it more important than my serenity?" Interesting: the *situation* doesn't change, but my *perception* of the situation changes.

One of the most effective communication skills I've learned has to do with Rule 62. Look it up! ***Rule 62*** in the Twelve Steps and Twelve Traditions, Tradition Four, says, "Don't take yourself so damned seriously." My sponsor gave me this example of my importance: take a glass of water and stick your finger in it, then pull your finger out of the water. The hole that remains in the glass of water is how important I am.

We began to lighten up and *not* take ourselves so seriously. In our relationship, *we were separate and independent people.* We began to give each other *the right to be right and the right to be wrong. We began to want our partners to be the best they could be.* **This is autonomy. This is true, other-centered love.**

Autonomy is another word for "**emotional detachment.**" Emotional detachment involves detaching ***only*** *emotionally* and ***only*** *from the* **problem** – not from the **person***.* That is so important. In "The Courage to Change," one of the daily readings states: "I discovered I don't have to react just because I have been provoked, and I don't have to take harsh words to heart. I remember that they come from someone who may be in pain, and I try to show compassion. Certainly, I don't have to allow them to provoke me into anything I don't want to do. ***Detachment with love*** means I stop depending on what others do, say, or feel to determine **my own** well-being or to make my decisions. When faced with other people's destructive attitudes and behavior, *I can love their best and never fear their worst.*"

This beautiful passage points out that there are only two emotions at play when we ***respond*** to life: I can respond to life with either ***love*** or ***fear. That's it.*** Before getting sober, my entire life, before I drank, during my drinking days, and after I quit drinking, I was driven by "a hundred forms of fear." In A.A, I have learned to base my ***actions*** on love rather than fear. The motive of love is *always* the right motive, and if I operate from this base of love and leave the results up to God, I believe things turn out the way they're supposed to, even if it's not the way I want them to turn out! Our co-founder, Dr. Bob, said that the whole A.A. program can be summed up in the words **"love and service."**

The fear of losing disappeared when reacting in love became more important to me than the ever-present need to win at any cost. I've learned to ask the question: "What is the loving thing to do?" when faced with indecision about what to do next.

On days when I am spiritually fit, I've learned to communicate this message: "I love and accept you as you are today, right now. I'm 100% committed to our relationship; your happiness is important. I will not try to change you; that's not my job. My responsibility is to fit *me* to be of maximum service."

By the way, this does ***not*** mean being a doormat! ***All of what we've been talking about concerns my attitude*** about myself, God, and others. Actually, it is about life itself. I've been taught that my ***thoughts*** are *energy*. When my thoughts are good, the good gets better, and vice-versa. I chased happiness my whole life and never found it until I came to Alcoholics Anonymous and discovered that happiness is not a *goal. Happiness is a by-product of doing the next right thing right.* Happiness is an *attitude,* and I am the only one responsible for my attitude. I'll never forget my feeble attempts at writing a gratitude list when I was newly sober. I couldn't think of a single thing to be grateful for. My sponsor had to help me. The first thing she suggested was the gratitude I felt for being sober! Today, there's not enough paper in the world to contain my gratitude list! As I said earlier, for *our* purposes, the Fourth Tradition could read: "Each person should be autonomous in the relationship except in matters affecting each other, the relationship itself, or others in our lives." "Autonomy" means "self-governing." Each partner is self-governing unless it affects each other, the relationship, or others.

As God's children and under his loving guidance, autonomy also means responsibility, the responsibility to protect the integrity of the relationship. *I had an epiphany:* I had to look at *me and my* old ideas (not Bill and his old ideas, which were *obviously wrong*). My old ideas were a solid *core* of long-buried and **unexamined** beliefs formed in childhood and based on my *perceptions.* I needed to find out through examination of *all* my old ideas that *some* of my old ideas were right and appropriate, such as being financially responsible, but that most of my old ideas weren't conducive to a healthy relationship.

As you can see from what I've already described, I looked at the world through my unique pair of glasses. These glasses were made up of culturally inherited qualities, family influences, and life experiences. These glasses determine what *I* bring to any relationship. I needed a change in *perspective, a new pair of glasses.* I couldn't *think* my way into it with the same thinking that got me into A.A. ***I had to do to be. I had to do something, not think something!*** In my case, it was usually doing something I didn't *feel* like doing – something beyond my comfort zone.

I know I've told you about this before, but the best example I can give you of action-changing thoughts is the exercise our sponsors suggested we do every night for what seemed like forever. In the beginning, we both felt embarrassed and uncomfortable. We had to sit knee to knee, holding hands and inviting God into our discussion. We would say the serenity prayer *out loud* and begin to talk, *taking turns*. I *had* to listen to him. I couldn't interrupt or criticize him. I *had* to listen politely.

He had to do the same thing. I could not "fix" him. He could not "fix" me. I could only talk about how *I* felt and work through *my* fear of being vulnerable. **Intimacy is really sharing from the heart without being judged.** I read that somewhere.

This repetitive knee-to-knee exercise changed our thoughts and feelings about each other and our relationship. By the way, the more we practiced this exercise, the more comfortable we felt doing it. The embarrassment left us, and it became one of our communication exercises.

The whole idea of communication is to enable the other person to *hear* what we are actually *saying*. I can still remember telling a woman I sponsored, "I know what I am saying; I *don't* know what you are hearing."

When I judge or criticize (always *negatively*, by the way), I'm building a wall between you and me. I'm saying I'm superior to you and know what is right and wrong *for you*. I'm saying you are an *extension of me*, not an independent entity. I'm saying I know better than you how you should think and feel, how you should dress and drive, and spend your money and your time.

This is true whether the relationship is between husbands and wives, parents and grown children, friends, co-workers, people we sponsor, or the person with 21 items in the 20-item line at the grocery store.

As God's children and under his loving guidance, we began to be willing to take the actions necessary to protect the *integrity* of our relationship. Sometimes, I take loving action even when I don't believe it, don't think it is a good idea, and don't even *feel* like it!

Slowly, the "We" became more important than the "You" or the "I." *Integrity* and *mutually agreed-upon unity* are two ethical principles that became goals for both of us. When you think about it, the primary message of the Big Book can be summed up in this sentence from Step Nine: "Our real purpose is to fit ourselves to be of maximum service to *God and the people about us.*" Check out the Third and Seventh Step prayers: in the Third Step prayer, we ask God to help us change in order to *be more useful to the people we help*. "Take away my difficulties that victory over them may bear witness to *those I would help*." In the Seventh Step prayer: "I pray that you now remove from me every single defect of character which stands in the way of my *usefulness to you and my fellows*." Even the last page (164) in our Big Book says: "*Ask God in your morning meditation what you can do each day for the man who is still sick.*"

What a shock to find out that in order to be spiritually fit, this principle must be applied **with courtesy** to *everyone*, including husbands and wives! It applies to *everyone* I come in contact with, including friends, co-workers, neighbors, acquaintances, children, parents, department store clerks, people in line at the grocery with 21 items in a 20-item line, slow drivers, and the list goes on. Autonomy means *self-governing*. It also means *responsibility*. How do *my* actions affect the relationship as a whole? How does this affect *us*, not how does it affect *me*?

You have probably noticed that I use a lot of repetition in this workshop to make my point. I have come to believe that repetition is how the message gets down into my unconscious mind and replaces the old ideas that are so self-defeating. This is how I incorporate the new learning so it becomes part of me.

Here's an example of what I mean. Why do you think we read "How It Works" and the Traditions aloud at every A.A. meeting? I'll bet most of you know it by heart because you have heard it so many times.

I did this calculation recently. Let's see; I've been sober for 48.25 years. I think I've averaged four meetings a week over the years. There are 2,509 weeks in 48.25 years. *So that means I have heard "How It Works," and the Traditions read 12,106 times.* 12,106 times! Imagine what else I've listened to 12,106 times.

I remember in early sobriety when my sponsor would tell me some A.A. wisdom for the umpteenth time. I would think, "She has told me this A.A. wisdom umpteen times now. *I get it."* The funny thing is, Tommie has been gone for a few years, and I am so grateful that I hear her voice in my head saying these same wise things that, in my arrogance, I used to get annoyed with. She is still guiding me towards love and service.

What geniuses our founders were to break down the concept of *change* into bite-sized pieces. They knew we could do *anything* for one day. They knew this because *they* were capable of taking new actions for one day! The old timers said, "By the inch, it's a cinch. By the yard, it's hard."

I *love* silly stuff like this because it's the truth!

Chapter Four

Questions from Tradition Four

1. *How do I understand and honor the concept of "unity" in any group of two or more?*

2. *How am I willing to stay in the relationship with the goal of growth in that relationship?*

3. *Have I made that 100% commitment to my partner?*

4. *How am I autonomous (self-governing) in my relationships?*

5. *Have I made my partner my higher power? If yes, why?*

6. *Have I made other people or other things my higher power? If yes, why?*

7. *Am I my higher power? Ouch!*

8. *What is the difference between caregiving and caretaking? Am I a caretaker or a caregiver? Examine each premise. Where do I fit in?*

9. *Am I looking outside myself for peace and contentment? How? Why?*

10. *Do I expect others to change so I'll feel better? Do they?*

11. *Do I define myself as a victim, or do I see that I am a volunteer most of the time?*

12. *Do I examine my "old ideas" about the right/wrong way to do things and discuss these perceptions with my sponsor and my partner as they crop up in our day-to-day relationships?*

13. *How am I willing to work hard to improve my communication skills?*

14. *Am I willing to learn to communicate assertively? What does that mean?*

15. *Do I react?*

16. *Do I forget my 12-step program in the heat of battle?*

17. *Do I fight aggressively? What does that mean?*

18. *Do I fight passively, even if it means feeling angry inside? What does that look like? What am I afraid of if I react assertively?*

19. *Do I insist "they" are making me feel this way?*

20. *Do I develop a long list of "shoulds" for others and myself? ("You should...")*

21. *Do I pout?*

22. *Do I insist that if they loved me, they should be able to read my mind?*

23. *Do I get angry at someone and take out my anger on something other than that person? Other people? The dog? What does that look like?*

24. *Do I run away? Do I sleep on the couch? Do I practice the silent treatment?*

25. *Do I become the victim? Am I a martyr?*

26. *Do I justify my position about everything? Why?*

27. *Do I get defensive? What does this look like?*

28. *Do I interrupt? Do I interrupt to judge or criticize? Why?*

29. *What message am I communicating when I negatively judge or criticize?*

30. *Do I complain back **at** them if they complain about something I did or said?*

31. *Do I try to "fix" my partner or anyone else? Do I want someone to "fix" me?*

32. *Do I respond?*

33. *Do I acknowledge their right to their feelings even if I disagree?*

34. *Am I willing to practice "active listening?" Am I willing to learn the techniques of active listening?*

35. *What is active listening?*

36. *Do I check my communication skills in difficult conversations to see if that is really where the problem lies?*

37. *Do I neglect my 12-step program during difficult times, saying, "I don't have time to go to a meeting; I have to sit here and think about my difficult times!"*

38. *Am I willing to learn and practice "emotional detachment?" What does that mean?*

39. *Do I respond to life with love or fear? Why?*

40. *Do I still make a daily gratitude list?*

41. *Do I practice "Rule 62" in my relationships? What is Rule 62?*

Primary Purpose!

TRADITION FIVE IN the 12 x 12 states: "Each group has but one primary purpose – to carry its message to the alcoholic who still suffers."

Tradition Five in relationships could be stated this way: A relationship has but one primary purpose – to build a strong and healthy relationship, ensuring that we are both on the same page and working toward the same goals. Personal relationships should support and encourage each other, creating a strong sense of unity and purpose. Our primary purpose is to love one another in a healthy fashion and carry this message to others.

How do we do this? We're learning through the Traditions how to have healthy personal relationships.

We carry the message when we incorporate an attitude of love and tolerance and deliver it to everyone we meet. Every encounter forms a relationship, no matter how brief or fleeting. Carrying the message embodies the most basic concept of Alcoholics Anonymous: **helping others**. Notice how vague that concept is. "**Helping**." In what way?

How much? When? Look at "**Others**." Who are they? Only alcoholics? Only people?

Our program is riddled with hints about our real purpose in life, but they all boil down to "Love and Service." That's what our co-founder, Dr. Bob Smith, said. If selfishness and self-centeredness are the root of my problem, other-centeredness, God-centeredness, is the solution.

As a child of God, I want my partner, friend, child, coworker, woman I sponsor, the stranger I sit next to on an airplane, the person with 21 items in the 20-item line, slow drivers – *I want each to be their best.* I want to encourage their mental, emotional, and spiritual growth. I mean *everyone* I come in contact with! "God, help me to treat others the way I want to be treated."

My own mental, emotional, and spiritual growth must gradually increase to attain this attitude. Progress, not perfection, right?

Growing up, because I was a fear-based child, I viewed everyone I met with suspicion and animosity. I judged and criticized everyone. I defined the world as a dangerous place and allowed no one to see the real me. (I think perhaps I didn't even let *me* see the real me!)

When I came into A.A., I slowly began to change as I realized that you were comfortable being honest in front of me, and it was *safe* for me to do the same.

My sponsor put it this way: "We come into A.A. encased in a solid block of ice because we feel so badly about ourselves. As we work the program in the loving atmosphere of Alcoholics Anonymous, the ice begins to melt, our authentic selves are exposed, and we change how we think and feel about ourselves, the world, and its people."

Once again, ***I must act my way into good thinking; I can't think my way into good acting***. If I accept you as you are *at this moment* and operate from a non-judgmental position of unconditional love, I will not be threatened by you. I don't have to be afraid of you, nor do I have to dominate you to feel okay.

If I'm becoming secure in a loving relationship with my higher power, I can say, "God, help me treat others tomorrow *the way you treated me today*."

The Second Step says, "Came to believe," not "Came to believe by next Tuesday." No matter where I am in my spiritual growth, I can always adopt a new attitude, as hesitant as it might be.

If this is my approach to others, people don't become defensive. My sponsor told me that if I'm speaking from a position of love, not anger or defensiveness, I can say anything I need to say, although not necessarily what I *want* to say.

Our 12-Step program is a loving program. I should be able to show God's love to all I have contact with, especially those closest to me. It is easier to take this action when I remember that I suffer from the fatal malady of alcoholism and that my disease has damaged my spiritual and emotional development.

Accepting this reality helps me to be more gentle in my treatment of the other person.

Above everything, I need to be careful not to demand that your growth be what I think it should be based on *my* beliefs and skewed perceptions. I could see precisely how Bill should change and how happy he would be when he became the person I knew he should be! However, *he* didn't quite see it that way!

Here's something to think about: *I don't see things as they are; I see things as I am.* **What I'm looking for, I'm**

looking with. I'm always looking for confirmation of my beliefs. For example, Charlie P. says, "I have found myself reading the Big Book and unconsciously looking for the things I've agreed with in previous readings." I nod my head and say, "Yes, that's right," as I read along familiar territory. I'm not looking for *new* information or ideas; I'm looking to confirm my *old* ideas. This is also true in my daily life. If I look out through angry, selfish eyes, I will see angry, selfish people and then react *as if that were true!*

Isn't it funny how I create *new* old ideas in A.A.? And like the *old*, old ideas, I'm unaware of them until the disparity between the old idea and *reality* becomes painful enough for me to acknowledge it!

One of my favorite poets, Anais Nin, says it this way:

> "And the day came when the risk to remain
> tight in a bud was more painful than the risk it
> took to blossom."

The Traditions are an invitation to re-think all my old ideas and my *new* old ideas!

The Traditions encourage us to see and live life in a new light. I cannot escape my unconscious biases except through a spiritual awakening. My *experience* tells me this spiritual growth usually involves pain. The *pain* comes from my resistance to change and not letting go of old ideas. Once I let go, there is no more pain.

Bill and I had always prayed together morning and night, even before our marriage, but now we began to pray together about our *relationship*. Our prayers solidified the fact that we were in this deal together. We were 100% committed to the unity of our marriage, no matter what. Our prayers brought about positive changes as we heard *each other* ask God for help. This was such a healthy process!

Even though we might be embroiled in a *war of egos* ten minutes later, our persistence in our prayers had a cumulative effect. Our disagreements became less heated, the duration of our fights lessened, and the time in between arguments lengthened.

St. Francis' prayer became our "To-Do list." That prayer and Tradition Five ask us to give others understanding, comfort, and encouragement. It says nothing about "except when I feel righteous anger, judgment, or criticism."

One of the hardest things for me to learn was that sometimes other people say things that I interpret **personally** as mean or hurtful when it is really about what is going on with *them*, not me. This was such a significant shift in my thinking and perspective. Our Big Book says, "We are sensitive people; it takes some of us a long time to outgrow this."

For many years, I had operated on the premise that *everything was about me.* What a shock to find out that sometimes I'm not even part of the equation. We all know the story of the man who had a hard day at work, came home, and kicked the dog. It had nothing to do with the dog, although the dog probably thought it was; *it had to do with the man.* But the dog (**me**) spent the rest of the evening this way:

- Wondering what she had done wrong;
- Anxiously thinking of ways to get the man not to be mad at her;
- Getting resentful at the man because he had utterly ruined her evening, made her feel awful, and was responsible for everything that had gone wrong that day;
- **In her head,** she won the argument. **In her head,** he apologized.
- She felt better.

Our trouble centers in our minds...

Once I figured out (with the help of my sponsor, of course) that sometimes communication can come out sideways, I could step aside from the notion that I was being personally attacked and put my focus on the *other person,* saying to myself, "This is a sick man. God, show me how I can be helpful to him." I could then show the other person compassion rather than defensive anger. I must admit that in the beginning, I took a great deal of secret pleasure in defining Bill as a "sick man." There was the unspoken conclusion that I wasn't sick!

Asking, "What's *really* going on?" is an excellent way to start a conversation. If I ask lovingly, the other person does not necessarily raise their defensive wall, angrily declaring, "Nothing! I'm FINE," and walking away.

If the relationship is based on mutual love and unity, they are more apt to sigh with relief and begin to talk honestly: "Well, at work today...." My job is to listen patiently without criticism or interruption.

That "listening" thing sounds so simple. I always thought I knew how to listen—I've been doing it all my life. No, I learned there is a difference between self-involved listening and genuine hearing. Genuine hearing requires *empathy* and *compassion*.

Becoming a good listener requires practice. It is a learned skill, not automatic. I heard "learn to listen and listen to learn" when I first entered A.A. There is a difference between *really listening and waiting for my turn to talk*. When thinking about what I will say next while the other person is talking, I am trying to *hi-jack* the conversation, especially if I'm about to give unsolicited advice. It is a form of **bullying**. I am arrogantly trying to control what the other is feeling and thinking. I am saying, "I know better than you how to live your life." I'm saying, "I'm going to fix you," implying that you are broken.

Authentic listening is surrendering control and letting the story unfold. It is being in the present moment. Listening takes me out of myself and teaches me how to connect with others. It is authentic communication. Listening is done with more than our ears. Through patience and persistence, I learn to listen with my heart, not just my judgmental head.

Attentive listening is about respect for the other person; it shows I care. It shows you matter. *Authentic listening* is an act of love.

We listen to obtain information, understand, enjoy, and learn. However, we only retain 25 – 50% of what we hear. This can cause problems! Let's look at a technique called "*Active Listening.*"

I call it "Listening with the Third Ear." It is a learned technique.

Active listening is making a conscious effort to hear the words that another person is saying and the complete message the other person is communicating. To do this, you must carefully pay attention to the other person. You can't allow yourself to be distracted by whatever else is happening around you or by forming counterarguments while the other person is still speaking. Nor can you allow yourself to get bored or lose focus on what the other person is saying; you need to let the other person know that you are listening to what they are saying – a simple nod of the head can be acknowledgment. An occasional question or comment to recap what has been said also communicates that you are listening and understanding the message.

Five Key Active Listening Techniques

1. PAY ATTENTION

- Look at the speaker directly
- Put aside distracting thoughts
- Don't mentally prepare a rebuttal
- "Listen" to the speaker's body language

2. SHOW THAT YOU'RE LISTENING

Use your own body language and gestures to show you're engaged

- Nod occasionally
- Smile and use other facial expressions
- Make sure your posture is open
- Encourage the speaker to continue with small verbal comments

3. PROVIDE FEEDBACK

Our personal filters, assumptions, judgments, and beliefs can distort what we hear. To understand what is being said, you might need to reflect on what is being said and ask questions.

- *Paraphrase.* "What I'm hearing is...." "Sounds like you're saying..." is a great way to reflect.
- *Ask questions* to clarify specific points: "What do you mean by...."
- *Summarize* the speaker's comments periodically
- If you find yourself responding emotion-ally, say so. *Ask for more information.* "I may not be understanding you correctly, and I find myself taking what you said personally. What
- I thought you said is *XXX*. Is that what you meant?"

4. DEFER JUDGMENT

Interrupting is a waste of time. It frustrates the speaker and limits the complete understanding of the message.

- Allow the speaker to finish each point before asking questions
- Don't interrupt with counterarguments

5. RESPOND APPROPRIATELY

Active listening is designed to encourage respect and understanding. You add nothing by attacking the speaker and otherwise putting them down.

- Be candid, open, and honest in your response
- Assert your opinions respectfully
- Treat the other person the way you would like to be treated.

It takes a lot of concentration and determination to be an active listener. Old habits are hard to break, and if your listening skills are as bad as mine were, you'll need to do a lot of work to break these bad habits.

(Adapted from MINDTOOLS.COM)

So along with learning how to *fight fair*, Bill and I began to learn how to *listen* to each other as we sat, knee to knee, and took turns listening to each other.

This new training was beneficial to every area of my life. Can you imagine how much more effective my ability to sponsor became? Instead of waiting impatiently for a woman to stop talking so I could give her the benefit of my incredible wisdom (read: opinion, judgment, advice), I **actively listened** to what she was saying, detached myself **emotionally** from what she was saying, and *objectively* could **hear** what she was saying. To me, being *lovingly objective* is a large part of good sponsorship, but I have to be able to really *hear* what the other person is saying to know what to be objective about!

As I "listen to learn and learn to listen," I discovered an additional benefit: *I had a great memory!*

It turns out I wasn't really forgetful, as I had always thought; I never heard what was being said in the first place! I believe that I pay attention to what is important to me, and if I'm selfish and self-centered, you and your life are not important to me. Active listening is about respect for the other person. It shows I care. It shows you matter. Authentic listening is an act of love. Genuine concern for what is happening in and with the other person without regard for my self-obsessed thoughts and feelings is a clear example of St. Francis' Prayer and the Fifth Tradition. It is how I want others to feel about me.

My real purpose is to fit myself to be of maximum service to God and the people about me. In my persistent efforts to approach this goal, I believe that God is doing for me what I could not do for myself.

The Fifth Tradition asks us to give others understanding, comfort, and encouragement. When I can take these loving actions, I feel good about myself in a simple *self-esteemy* way! By encouraging another's recovery, I am working towards my own.

My self-esteem is based on doing esteemable actions. *I have to do to be* (isn't that worth pondering?). When I ask God to let me see the other person through *His* eyes rather than my own, I become willing to be loving. Initially, it felt awkward to be warm and fuzzy when I was used to being bristly and cold. Since I had no idea how to be *genuinely* warm and fuzzy, I began asking other people I knew were loving people how to be loving! I started to practice this concept on *"safe"* people: the women in the A.A. meetings I attended, the clerk in the drugstore, the postman, and especially my sponsor!

As time went on, my persistence paid off. I was practicing love while feeling awkward doing it.

A.A. is about walking from the Prosecution table to the Defense table. How different it looks from there! I can see things from *their* viewpoint, giving me a new perspective. This is really hard when dealing with the resentments on our Fourth Step list or close family members. Trying this technique on people we interact with once is easier and more fun: a clerk at the grocery store who is rude to me. I think, "What a pity. His dog is sick, and he must be at work instead of home with his sick dog." Of course, I have no idea what's happening to his dog, or even if he has a dog, but *changing how I think changes how I feel.* This is valid for any encounter, no matter how seemingly insignificant. This is especially helpful when I find myself behind really slow drivers – in this case, they're taking their sick dog to the vet and are looking for the road to turn for the vet's office.

From competitive misery and failure, Bill and I began to find love and joy in each other as separate but connected human beings. Happiness was a by-product of working the Steps and Traditions into our daily lives. Our relationship became deeper, less combative, and less superficial. It became more authentic and more rewarding for each of us.

Here's a suggestion: if you are in this workshop as an individual, go out and practice what you've learned with friends, family, clerks in the grocery store – and other people. If you are reading this book as a couple, take the individual notes you might have taken during the previous chapters or the *"Questions from the Traditions,"* and each person read your notes or answers to the other person. Sit knee to knee, facing each other – *you know the drill.*

Sometimes your notes will be different, or the answers to the questions will differ. Discussing the answers and commenting on how these things relate to the two of you is helpful.

For example, "What are we doing in this area, and what must we do to improve?" This question reinforces what you're trying to learn and encourages you to incorporate these Traditions into your daily lives.

The Fifth Tradition teaches us how to convey a message of love and tolerance, mercy and compassion to others. Each relationship has but one primary purpose: to love one another and serve as an expression of God's love.

It sounds so simple. To do this, I had to learn how to communicate and listen authentically. This required humility, guidance, and a new way of thinking about everyone I encountered during the day. The reward of doing so is the peace I had been looking for my whole life. At last, I had a way to achieve this peace.

Chapter Five

Questions from Tradition Five

1. *Is my primary purpose to develop a healthy attitude of love and service and to carry this message to others?*

2. *Do I have to give it away to keep it, even if it only involves being an example? How do I do this?*

3. *Do I believe every direct encounter with another person is a relationship, no matter how fleeting? (Ranging from lifelong partner to two minutes with a grocery store clerk)*

4. *In all my relationships, do I support and encourage the other person's mental, emotional, and spiritual growth? How do I do this?*

5. *What do I mean when I say, "What I'm looking for, I'm looking with?"*

6. *Do I ask God to help me treat others tomorrow the way he treated me today?*

7. *Do I demand that your growth be what **I** think it should be based on **my** beliefs and perceptions? Why?*

8. *Do I give advice to others, or do I offer **only** the spiritual principles of A.A. and my experience, strength, and hope?*

9. *Do I accept others as they are at this moment, knowing they will grow and change just as I do? If not, why not?*

10. *Do I practice unconditional love? What does this mean?*

11. *In what way is practicing unconditional love different from being a passive doormat?*

12. *Do I make a daily gratitude list? Do I make a daily gratitude list about my partner and other important people in my life?*

13. *Do I understand the relationship between Tradition Five and the Saint Francis prayer?*

14. *How do I express God's love to others?*

15. *With my partner, am I compassionate rather than defensive? Do I realize it's not always about me, me, me?*

16. *Have I walked from the Prosecution table to the Defense table? What does this mean?*

17. *What is the difference between listening and hearing?*

18. *Is listening a learned skill? What does this mean?*

19. *Do I listen to my partner, or am I thinking about what I will say while my partner is talking? Do I hi-jack conversations? How?*

20. *Do I practice ACTIVE LISTENING? What are the five key active listening techniques?*

21. *Is my happiness a goal or a by-product of living the A.A. way of life?*

Unity Matters!

IN THE 12 x 12, Tradition Six states: "An A.A. group ought never endorse, finance or lend the A.A. name to any related facility or outside enterprise, lest problems of money, property, and prestige divert us from our primary purpose."

Tradition Six in our *personal* relationships might read as follows: "There must be singleness of purpose in any relationship, no matter how fleeting because money, property, and prestige can divert us from our primary spiritual purpose. Our primary spiritual purpose is to love one another and to serve as an expression of God's love.

We are all doing the best we can according to our understanding of our lives. I'm not the same person I was yesterday. I'm the same person I was yesterday, *plus* yesterday's experiences and my *interpretation* of those experiences.

I came into A.A. because I surrendered to my powerlessness; I was a broken human being, a nothing. As time went on in sobriety, I became *somebody*. When you're *somebody*, you have rights – when you have rights, you must defend them. I believe that the God of my experience loves me enough to allow me to make my own mistakes so that I run out of my own resources ("Captain Self-Reliant," that was me) and come back home where I belong.

When I was seven years sober, I almost left Alcoholics Anonymous and *didn't even know it.* I didn't wake up one morning and declare, "I've learned all I need to know – I think I'll be fine without A.A." No, I was unaware of the slippery slope I was on. I live my life forward but understand it backward. Thinking about this event scares me even today.

Here's what happened. Bill and I married and were working on our "Marital Recovery Plan." Sometimes it was a bumpy ride. Now, I had begun to make amends to my body when I was a year sober, and physical exercise was part of those amends. During the troubled times of our early marriage, I unconsciously exercised more and more. I reveled in the many compliments about how great I looked. I was gaining prestige about me, me, me, and it felt good. This was in stark contrast to the criticism I received at home (we were still playing a bit of the "blame game"). I could think about my strong, healthy body rather than the mess I thought my marriage was in. I was completely unaware that I had become obsessed with exercise. Soon, I backed away from a favorite A.A. meeting because it was at the same time as a particular aerobics class I wanted to attend. I had already begun to criticize the format of that A.A. meeting and the quality of the sobriety in that room. I found fault with the women in that meeting and stopped going for coffee and fellowship afterward. This continued till I was only going to one meeting a week. Interestingly enough, that one meeting was one that my sponsor attended, and I certainly didn't want *her* to know what I was doing (we're as sick as our secrets, right?). I told myself she was old, she wouldn't understand!

I was still sponsoring women, of course. After all, I had so much quality sobriety to share! One day, *between* exercise classes, I was sitting in a diner, pontificating my wisdom to a woman I sponsored. Out of the corner of my eye, I unexpectedly saw *my* sponsor in her car at the drive-through. Suddenly, like a lightning bolt, and with great clarity, I saw what I was doing. There's a line in Step 10, "Alcohol is a subtle foe." *I felt it. I felt it down to my toes.* I ran out of the restaurant to Tommie's car. "I'm in trouble," I cried. "Let's get together and talk about it," she calmly said. That evening, I went to her house and surrendered *again* to my powerlessness. I had allowed personal prestige and self-centeredness to divert me from the essential part of my primary purpose: *staying sober*. It was my second surrender, deep and profound.

I surrendered to my **powerlessness** over alcohol *and* the *unmanageability* of my own life **sober**. I surrendered to the fact that *powerlessness is not an event; it is a condition!* AND the dash is there in the First Step to extend the admission of powerlessness to include my *thinking.* My addictive thinking is behind my unmanageability. It's a perception problem. The scary part is that I had been completely blinded to the fact that I was in relapse. I had not thought of drinking yet, but I was setting myself up for it. Alcohol is a subtle foe – so is my thinking!

Life takes place between my ears. Think about it. Alcoholic *thinking* doesn't stop when I stop alcoholic *drinking*. I had to stop thinking I could solve my thinking problem with my thinking. I had believed that once I was sober, I could manage my life, and it was only unmanageable while I was drinking! Another line from the Big Book applies here: "We suffered under the delusion that we could wrest satisfaction and happiness out of this world if we only managed well."

"Wrest" means "to seize with force." I had tried to "wrest" happiness out of self-centered prestige because working to have a healthy relationship in my marriage, my "group of two," was so painful. This distraction from my primary purpose put me at risk of losing my sobriety and, of course, my marriage.

This second surrender changed my life. Nothing had actually changed, but everything was different. I had a new pair of glasses. I looked at my world from an entirely different angle. I resumed my regular A.A. meeting schedule and exercise became a *part* of my life, not *all* of my life. I returned to the hard work of forging a healthy relationship with my husband and the other people in my life. I got out of the driver's seat.

I turned my life and will back over to the God of my experience.

I still had the human problem of emotional immaturity. I had admitted I didn't know how to have a healthy relationship. I began to consult with others who did know how to have healthy relationships. This involved my sponsor, Bill's sponsor, some healthy friends, and the occasional therapist.

In the past chapters, I've written about *listening skills*. I've written about *fair fighting*. I've written about *communication skills*. Books about relationships were helpful. They usually gave specific illustrations and directions. Nowadays, with Amazon, Google, and the rest of the Internet, there's no end to the information and suggestions available to us.

Prestige and money were among the most significant stumbling blocks for me. I've told you about my ill-advised excursions into prestige-seeking. What about money issues? Bill and I were fiscally responsible people, but we did have different beliefs that caused friction in our house. We found out that *money* was not the issue; it was our different *feelings* about money and the lack of clear communication **about** money that caused the problem. There are experts on financial management, books to read, and courses to take. Dave Ramsey is one of the best-known experts on financial matters. Google Dave Ramsey's "The Seven Baby Steps" for beginner's information and suggested guidance. This will probably lead to further research, as it did for Bill and me.

The need for honest communication and a willingness to compromise is the most significant hot-button issue among couples, not the money itself. This can include problems between parents and teenage children, girlfriends dividing up the check at lunch, and members of an A.A. group at a business meeting.

Money can be an emotional issue – a personal issue.

Quarrels and resentments can flourish. Underneath every disagreement is fear. Fear that we'll lose something we have or not get something we want. Each of us emotionally distorts the facts to manage our fears. It will be a life-long job to overcome the fears that drive us, alcoholic or not, and we will probably never be completely free of fear. We will attack or withdraw when we feel threatened or insecure, according to our habitual way of dealing with fear. I am a sneaky attacker, usually in an underhanded, manipulative way. As a partner or individual, I must become aware of the *self-deception* that powers my fears. This is where sponsors, the Twelve Steps, and the Twelve Traditions come into play and get us back on track. To be free, I must learn how to communicate honestly and *prioritize* the welfare of my group. We have a primary purpose: to have a unified partnership, to love one another, and to serve as an expression of God's love. We must crawl out of self-centeredness and find spiritual answers and the peace that comes from these spiritual answers.

Issues of money, property, and prestige are just manifestations of our basic trouble, self-centered fear, and the program of Alcoholics Anonymous, when it is practiced as a way of life, can pull us *out* of this swamp of fear as individuals and as partners, in a group of two or a group of twenty-two.

A little sign on my desk says: *Good morning! This is God, and I will be handling all your problems today. I will not need your help. So relax and have a great day!"*

Chuck C. says, "I got here knowing I had lost the battle of life. I had given it my all, and I had lost. So I can't run my own life. I've found I don't *need* to run my own life. I live in total expectation of guidance and direction, so I don't need to run my own life."

I needed to tap into something more powerful than my mind. I came to believe and trust that God will guide my thinking, restoring me to sanity.

Surrender happens when I change my behavior. It happened on the first night of my sobriety when I followed the suggestion of a sober woman in A.A. I got on my knees and asked something I didn't believe in to keep me away from one drink of alcohol that night This action showed a *willingness* brought about through the despair and loneliness of the drinking alcoholic.

One of the easiest ways to see the change in me is to look at how I sponsor. And, by the way, with my new-found humility because of my near-relapse, I became a better sponsor. *I'm just the vessel; I'm not the well.* I asked God to help me *not* be the know-it-all who needed to lecture or give advice on every subject, *not* to be in charge of everyone and everything.

I wrote in Tradition Four about the many dependencies I created, which crippled me and kept me from the Sunlight of the Spirit. My mind fought me every step of the way. It's used to being boss. *My mind is a bully.* It wants its own way. It wants to win at any cost. I read somewhere that the mind is a long-term habit that is not easily broken.

These *dependencies* I created, this kind of *emotional entanglement*, can overwhelm my primary purpose and the concept of unity in all its many forms. I can get pretty tangled up getting involved in things that are none of my business. I'm a fixer, and I have difficulty *not* getting involved.

I was at a meeting early in my sobriety and heard a speaker say, **"I have to act my way into good thinking; I can't think my way into good acting."** It would seem that my *actions* would determine whether I would stay sober, not my thoughts or feelings. In the beginning, I didn't have to believe in God to pray. In the beginning, I prayed to "A.A.'s" God. I was told I did not have to *feel* like going to a meeting; I just had to go. I was told I did not have to *feel* like working the Twelve Steps and Twelve Traditions into my life to do it. I just had to do it. A.A. is an *action* program. I don't have to understand it, figure it out, believe it, or approve of it to do it. I have to do it. Strangely, I began to *want* to follow directions – what a gift from a Power I was starting to believe in and trust. The results in my life were miraculous.

The evidence of the existence of God appears to us *through the process of believing.* We must always go beyond our ego-driven minds and surrender to the simple premise that *our understanding* of God will come from our *experience* of this power in our lives.

Here's an example: I realized that I began to know that a power outside of me cared about me when I had been sober for about three or four months without any effort on my part, without the white knuckling I always had to use in the past when I tried to quit drinking. I was amazed at this realization. How could this be? I had tried to control or moderate my drinking for three long years – *with my thinking.* I didn't know that Chapter Three of our Big Book describes almost everything I tried. I thought I was so unique! The *awareness* of a miracle in my life changed my thinking about a "power outside myself" more than anything else. I had concrete proof!

So what does this have to do with living the Traditions in our relationships?

Everything.

As a newcomer, I believed I could not form a true partnership with another human being. My sponsor pointed out that I was the common denominator in all my failed relationships. I had been married and divorced three times by the time I crawled into A.A. I had other troublesome relationships as well: I had parents, so I was an adult child; I had a daughter, so I was a parent, and I had friends over the years, so I was a friend. I had worked a little, so I was a worker, and, of course, I had been married, so I was an ex-wife. The problem was that I had *unknowingly* been self-centered in every one of my relationships – in my marriages, as a child, as a parent, as a friend, and at work. My sponsor assured me I would learn to have a different relationship because I would ask *God* to mold my ideas and establish new values.

I had been raised to believe that if anything was going to change in my life, I had to make the changes. "If it is to be, it's up to me." "No," my sponsor said, "You and your willpower can't do this job. If you could have accomplished this miracle, you would have done so long ago and wouldn't need the program of Alcoholics Anonymous." How would this transformation take place if *I* couldn't make the changes? "The Twelve Steps and Twelve Traditions," she said. They weren't just something to look at on the wall of a meeting room when I was bored; they were *actions* I would have to take to allow this higher power to change my life. "Oh, by the way," she said, "I'll meet you at the women's meeting Wednesday night." "Oh no," I cried, "I don't like women – they are either competition or stupid." Tommie smiled sweetly and said she would meet me at the women's meeting. Fear of sponsor overcame what I found out was really a fear of women. I could manipulate men, but I knew women could see right through me.

My *relationship therapy* began at that women's meeting. The meeting was on a Wednesday, and I started dreading it on Tuesday, but after a few meetings, I walked out one night saying, "That wasn't so bad – *they're* getting better!" But here is what was really happening: At my sponsor's suggestion, instead of everything being about me, me, me, I began to listen to these women – they became *real* people, and I began to identify with them. With my sponsor's guidance, I learned to ask them about *their* lives and stopped telling them about me, me, me, and *my* life. I remembered (because I wrote it down) that someone's daughter was graduating from high school, and I could ask her about the graduation. I remembered (because I wrote it down) asking how someone's sick husband was doing, the move into a new house, or how their dog liked the new doggie door. You get the idea – I was *so* self-centered it had never occurred to me that other people's lives were *important* to *them,* and showing an interest brought us closer. Soon I didn't have to write down the details; I really did care and remembered these things on my own. This is how the concept of *community* began for me.

I started to attend our monthly group-conscious meetings (some call them business meetings), and I saw that women could *disagree without being disagreeable!* There was no "win-lose" situation; it was all "win-win." There were no "bosses" in the group. Even those with many years in the program had no more influence than a newcomer like me. We were walking shoulder to shoulder. This was such a complex concept for me to grasp. However, I learned through the actions of teamwork in the women's meeting that I could walk shoulder to shoulder in *any* relationship – from the women in the meeting, my family, or the clerk in the grocery store.

Again, this Tradition protects the relationship *and* its unity. No one person can supply all the needs of another. We are responsible for taking care of ourselves and for having balance (humility) in our relationships. Our separateness is our mutual strength, promoting a partnership of healthy equals.

Another favorite poet, Kahlil Gibran, says it best:

On Marriage:

Let there be spaces in your togetherness
And let the winds of heaven dance between you.
Sing and dance together and be joyous, but let
each one of you be alone.

And stand together but not too near together,
For the pillars of the temple stand apart, and
the oak tree and the cypress grow not in each
other's shadow.

He defines in a few choice words what it will take me the rest of Tradition Six to talk about!

It has been my hard-learned, hard-earned experience that each partner should support the other spiritually, emotionally, and physically, but in a *balanced* fashion. In a *responsible* fashion. A grown-up person doesn't do for another what they can do for themselves.

Here's what I mean: in my life, I have always exhibited what I call the "*merge urge*," even though I was outwardly and defiantly self-reliant. I would meet someone, even as a child, attach myself to them like a barnacle, adopt their way of thinking and believing, and depend on them to totally take care of my needs in return for my undying loyalty. Undying till it wasn't.

I've told you about my "AHA" moment in sobriety when I realized that I had never made a 100% commitment to anything or anybody. With absolutely no thought for the feelings of the other, I'd turn my back and run.

This kind of thinking was only possible because I was 100% self-centered! I could only see others as a means of satisfying *my* needs and wants. As long as other people are actors on *my* stage, as long as they are only there to speak *my* lines and play the role *I* have assigned them – as the director in everyone's life, it's easy to dump them when they're no longer useful.

How arrogant and grandiose is that? It's easy to see why I call the women's meeting the best schoolroom I've ever had. I could learn how to have healthy, reciprocal relationships in a safe environment.

And yet, underneath the *arrogance* was a great *dependency*. I was totally dependent on these "actors" to play the roles and read the lines. I didn't want to be *unconditionally happy*. I wanted to be happy, **provided** I had the things I wanted. I had been taught to place my happiness in other people's hands. I suffered with an almost unconscious, ever-present *anxiety*, knowing that I had no real power to control those actors. In reality, *they* had the power, and I had given it to them! There's a saying I love: **Don't put the keys to your happiness in somebody else's pocket!**

Much later, in Alcoholics Anonymous, I ultimately gained the insight, the *awareness*, that these feelings were *inside of me*, not the other person. But as long as I believe it is *outside* of me, I am justified in holding onto my feelings, and in my mind, I am powerless. Before this awareness happened, the other person in my life became my *99% God* for the moment. My partner or friend became my crutch in life. I needed them to play *their* role so I could play mine! **This is not love; it is faulty dependency.** In A.A., I learned that there had to be a better way of living than *emotionally* depending on something outside myself for my sense of well-being. Only when I recognized this dependency did I become willing to challenge my whole belief system: beliefs about love, happiness, and the right and wrong way to do things.

I had been programmed – I had programmed *myself* – I didn't want to look at this belief system because if I did, I might have to *change*. I might learn something *new*. My first reaction to this possibility was fear. I read somewhere that this fear was not of the *unknown; I really feared* the loss of the *known* – the comfortable, familiar *known*.

I always *appeared* to accept the role of follower in my relationships. It never occurred to me to take a leadership role in my own life and end up where I wanted to be rather than where someone was taking me. I accepted the value system that said *other people's opinions of me were more important than my own opinions of myself*. I once read this statement: *"The bars of the strongest prison known to man are made up of the opinions of other people."* This is one of those old ideas that goes way back to childhood. I was completely unaware that there was no reaction in me that wasn't coming from someone else: not a thought, a belief, an attitude, a feeling – it was all coming from others I had long ago incorporated as "me." It would take a lot of pain for me to be willing to look at everything I'd built as "me" and see that it was a mixed bag of my experiences, my judgments, and most of all, the programming by others early in my life. The *resistance* to change, the clinging to the familiar, is painful. The more I resist something, the more power I give it.

To the extent that I give something else (*past or present, living or dead*) power over my feelings and my life, it is power *I have given them*. And I have learned in A.A. that I can take that power back anytime.

While I was *overly dependent*, I was at the same time a *control freak* in a very passive-aggressive way.

Two sides of the same coin.

When I feel I have no power *overtly*, I resort to *manipulation* and end up feeling bad about myself because I'm living a lie, thinking and feeling that I have no value as myself. So, **I look for it outside myself.**

This is such an insidious way of thinking and believing. Let me tell you of a situation I created when I was at least 20 years sober that illustrates what happens when I feel I have no power to get what I want: *I was in East Dorset, Vermont, at Wilson* house with my sponsor for a Women's Retreat. Tommie told me about an event that was to take place the following month in which she was invited to share and record her remembrances about her early years in A.A. (she got sober in 1961 in the northeast and knew a lot of the old-timers like Bill and Lois on a very personal level).

"That sounds wonderful," I said, "I'd like to go." She said, "You weren't invited." I asked about this event several times during the retreat, and each time, she repeated, "You weren't invited." I tried to *explain* to her how important it was to me to be there. I asked if I could go as her guest. "No, you were not invited," was all she said.

Without even knowing what was happening, my old tapes and my old ideas surfaced. I had no idea how dependent I was on Tommie to supply me with prestige and security that I didn't feel I deserved on my own. This recording session was a big deal in the A.A. community. If I could go with Tommie, *I* would be a big deal, too. I could brag about the event as though *I* was doing the recording! It would once again be about me, me, me! I wanted to go for my own immature reasons, having little to do with Tommie. Self-obsession was my underlying motivator. Of course, I was totally unaware of how my spiritual immaturity influenced and determined my behavior.

I had a *brilliant* "AHA" moment: a *plan* came into my head. I would call one of Tommie's best friends and get the phone number of the man who was arranging this recording event. I would explain who I was (Tommie's most important sponsee) and get an invitation to attend.

This I did, with complete success. I gleefully called Tommie to say, "I've been invited!" She didn't say much, but a few days later, she called. "Do you remember in your last Fourth Step, you said *manipulation* was still a major *character defect*? I just saw you demonstrate this in a big way." She said these words lovingly. A conversation followed; she never told me what to do or not do. We just explored the *thinking* about my need to get what I wanted when I wanted it and the *faulty dependency* on prestige gained from association with other people.

I made a grown-up decision: I called the host and withdrew from the invitation, then sulked at home for the whole weekend because I wasn't there! (I *told* you, my emotions and thinking are the last to catch up; my *behavior* has to change first!). My *behavior* at this point in my story was that of a grown-up!

So where was my healthy self-esteem in all this plotting and planning? Where was my emotional sobriety? Where was the loving, trusting relationship I had with Tommie? I was 20 years sober – I *should* be more advanced spiritually than this, right?

No. *My* path of spiritual recovery is *my* path, and there's no *A.A. yardstick to measure how I'm doing* – to see if I'm ahead or behind *you*, and *you* and *you*. God has no measuring stick, but I do!

Let's say I put a label on someone: "She's been sober for three years, and she's acting in a certain way." This carries an unspoken message of approval or disapproval, praise or blame – *according to me!* And it's *really* harsh when that judgment falls on me and how I "should" be according to a label I put on myself. I desperately needed to become aware of the labels of *dis*satisfaction I felt about myself, the competition, the comparisons, the "I'm not good enough," and the demands and expectations I put on *myself*. That was brutal!

Those "Shoulds" in my head are killers! It's me judging me by some *standard of perfection* I invented when I was seven years old. This *need to be perfect* creates a perfect *prison* where I *unconsciously* live my life. And then I will make it *your* fault when I fail to live up to *my* perfectionist standards.

It's funny, but I know that almost everyone with a few years in A.A. suffers from the "Shoulds." Do you? Can you locate and examine the "old ideas" that caused this character defect?

The other side of that coin is the need to be needed, my dependence on others for my legitimacy. This is such an indication of *low self-esteem!* My importance is validated by being needed. I have an over-developed sense of responsibility to help others. I play God. I become a caretaker rather than a caregiver. I learned the biggest, most powerful lessons about being dependent through *sponsorship – me* being the sponsor. I had yet to learn how much I needed to be needed by the women I sponsored. To be essential to their well-being, I had to be in charge, advise on all their life issues, and then make sure they *followed these directions.* If they didn't, I tried harder to convince them I was right. I was a "helper," a "fixer," and an enabler, creating sick dependencies in those I was trying to help. When they did follow my ubiquitous advice, I felt warm and fuzzy with the security of knowing I was being "helpful." I felt good because I was needed. I could visualize them at a podium getting their yearly medallion, thanking me for *saving their life*, and *owing their sobriety to me, me, me.*

It took me a while as a sponsor to realize I was placing my self-esteem in the hands of others, and if they rejected me or left my "care," *I felt worthless.*

I told you about one instance concerning a woman who **fired** me as her sponsor. I was seven years sober and *devastated. What would people think of me?* What would the other women I sponsored think of me? I wanted to hide, to move away and start over. I had no idea how dependent I was on other people's opinions to make me okay. I just knew I wanted to get away from the way I *felt.* (now *there's* a sentence I could elaborate on forever!). Repeat: *I wanted to get away from the way I felt!*

Slowly, and with Tommie's help, I began to see that, once again, I was victimized by my own dependencies. I began to see the underlying *ego-feeding* reasons for my need to control, the feelings of *personal unworthiness* that fed the need to control anything and everything.

I began to see that *sponsorship is not ownership*. I began to learn how to be a good and effective sponsor by detaching from the *need* to control the women I sponsor. *That need came from my own fear and was based on my own unhealthy self-esteem.*

Another beautiful "AHA" moment. From this new viewpoint, I began to examine the problems I had with my other relationships – my husband, my friends, my grown child, my co-workers – and *all* of my ongoing relationships.

I began to ask *God* to help me let go of my unhealthy dependence on *these* relationships as well. After all, it was about *me*, not them! This was good news: since the problem was in *me*, I didn't have to wait around for *them* to change so I'd feel better! I also began to see the *bigger picture*. I began to *want* to be more emotionally and spiritually independent.

As I stay sober and incorporate the spiritual program of Alcoholics Anonymous into my daily life, I am *changed*. My attitude, my perspective, and my outlook on life are transformed.

I was raised to present to the outside world *only* the *perfection* that I wanted others to believe about me – never anything I thought of as *shameful* (making a mistake) or *demeaning* (not knowing something, having a problem my self-reliance couldn't solve, or asking for help). This explains *my* unhealthy dependency on others to "supply me with security, prestige, and the like." I didn't have it on my insides; I had to get it from the *outside*, from *you*.

Bill Wilson writes: "If we examine every disturbance we have, great or small, we will find at the root of it some unhealthy dependency and its consequent, unhealthy demand," and, "Finally, we begin to see that *all* people, including ourselves, are to some extent emotionally ill as well as frequently wrong, and then we approach true tolerance and see what *real* love for our fellows actually means. It will become more and more evident as we go forward that it is pointless to become angry or get hurt by people who, like us, suffer from the pains of growing up."

That is why, as A.A. members, sponsors, and just plain old human beings, we learn to detach *emotionally* from these dependencies so that we can tend to our primary purpose.

The best part of being free and open to others is that I don't have to *pretend* anymore (that takes an enormous amount of energy). I don't have to remember what I said and to whom I said it! It cut way back on the anxiety I had lived with my whole life because I was living a lie and feared I could be exposed at any time. To paraphrase Bill Wilson: Now *my* brain no longer races compulsively in either elation, grandiosity, or depression. I, too, have been given a quiet place in bright sunshine

Questions from Tradition Six

1. *How am I an equal in my relationships – spiritually, mentally, and physically?*

2. *What is meant by "Our separateness is our mutual strength"?*

3. *Am I honest with my partner about doing what I need to do to be spiritually, emotionally, and physically self-supporting?*

4. *Am I in a relationship because I feel needed and, therefore, validated?*

5. *Am I in a relationship because I feel love for the other person and am loved by them?*

6. *Am I dependent on others for my legitimacy? Is my importance validated by being needed?*

7. *Do faulty dependencies victimize me? Explain.*

8. *Can I distinguish between healthy "support" and "enabling" someone? What is the difference?*

9. *Am I a care-taker or a care-giver?*

10. *Do I take responsibility for my own needs, or am I so busy caring for others that I neglect myself?*

11. *Do I "should" on myself? Can I locate, examine, and, if necessary, discard these "old ideas"?*

12. *Do I allow my grown children (and the people I sponsor) to be adults, or do I fix their problems, get them out of*

trouble, pay their financial obligations, and feel guilty because I am not a perfect parent?

13. *Have I learned to "detach emotionally with love" from my relationships?*

14. *Is emotional sobriety my next frontier?*

15. *What is emotional sobriety? Can I define it?*

16. *How will I get there?*

Support Matters!

EACH TRADITION EXPLAINS one specific way to protect the unity of the fellowship and the group. This applies to individual relationships as well.

In the 12 x 12, the Seventh Tradition reads: "Every A.A. group ought to be fully self-supporting, declining outside contributions."

For our purposes of examining and incorporating the Traditions in our daily relationships, the Seventh Tradition could read: "Each of us in the group ought to strive to be

fully and responsibly self-supporting spiritually, emotionally, and physically, establishing and maintaining appropriate
boundaries to protect and take care of ourselves and others.

That sounds complicated! So, let's break it down into
manageable pieces:

The Seventh Tradition suggests that we each strive to
be self-supporting through our own contributions. What
does this mean in a relationship? The dictionary defines
self-supporting as "maintaining oneself without reliance on
outside aid."

By the way, they're not talking about reliance on
the God of our understanding; they're talking about the
unbalanced, unhealthy dependence we develop on other
human beings for identification or existence.

This is true no matter what the relationship is, whether
it's for a reason, a season, or a lifetime.

A reason: someone comes into your life at a specific
time and for a purpose. The relationship ends when that
purpose is fulfilled. Example: I was out of town and had
received some bad news. I went to an A.A. meeting because
that's what we do when we're out of town and receive bad
news. I got a lot of comfort from that meeting, even though
I didn't say anything about the problem. After the meeting,
a woman approached me and asked if I'd like to walk to a
nearby café for coffee. While there, she asked me if I was

okay – I looked troubled in the meeting. I told her the entire story. She had had a similar experience and shared the solution her sponsor had suggested. It was perfect for my situation! I never saw her after that conversation. She was in my life for a reason, and we both knew it. We were two healthy individuals sharing a moment in time. She was, as they say, "God with skin on!"

A season: when I first got sober, I had to move from the little town of Palm Beach, Florida, to the big city of Ft. Lauderdale. I had to get a sponsor, and I did – for a season. The woman I chose was perfect for me at the time. She kept it simple, kept me in meetings, and introduced me to the women in the program. I was almost a year sober when she stopped attending meetings – she didn't drink, just stopped going to meetings, and I knew I had to get another sponsor. I found a wonderful woman who had the kind of sobriety I wanted. Her name was. Tommie. She was my sponsor for 42 years; she died in 2017 with 56 years of sobriety. You will read a lot of her wisdom throughout this writing and reminiscing.

A lifetime: When I was six years sober, I met a woman at a meeting who was a year sober. We clicked, and she asked me to be her sponsor. Forty years later, we are still in this "lifetime" relationship. Much of life has happened to us both during this time, but we've always cherished the connection. We have each taken the time and effort to maintain and grow our relationship. We are both 100% committed to our relationship!

I'm telling you all this because I came to A.A. with such screwy ideas about relationships: I used to think that every encounter was a life sentence. I have no idea where this idea came from, but I felt that if someone talked to me at the grocery store, I needed to keep in touch, and I felt mildly abandoned when the person said goodbye and left the store. This is an extreme example, but it shows how unbalanced I was in determining the importance of human interaction. It also shows how isolated I was and how I clung to any connection, any feeling of belonging.

On the flip side, I discounted and discarded essential relationships, like family, because I didn't want the *self-imposed anxiety* of ongoing relationships.

In the book "Adult Children of Alcoholics or Otherwise Dysfunctional Households," there is a list of characteristics of people who have grown up in dysfunctional families. See if you relate to any or all of them:

- We became isolated and afraid of people and authority figures.
- We became approval seekers and lost our identity in the process.

- We are frightened by angry people and any personal criticism.
- We either became alcoholics, married them, or both, or found another compulsive personality, such as a workaholic, to fulfill our sick abandonment needs.
- We live life from the viewpoint of victims and are attracted by that weakness in our love and friendship relationships.
- We have an overdeveloped sense of responsibility, and it is easier for us to be concerned with others rather than ourselves; this enables us not to look too closely at our own faults, etc.
- We get guilty feelings when we stand up for ourselves instead of giving in to others.
- We become addicted to excitement.
- We confuse love and pity and tend to "love" people we can "pity" and "rescue."
- We have "stuffed" our feelings from our traumatic childhoods and have lost the ability to feel or express our feelings because it hurts so much (Denial).
- We judge ourselves harshly and have a very low sense of self-esteem.
- We are dependent personalities who are terrified of abandonment and will do anything to hold onto a relationship in order not to experience painful

abandonment feelings, which we received from living with sick people who were never there emotionally for us.

Alcoholism is a family disease; we became para-alcoholics and took on the characteristics of that disease even though we did not pick up the drink.

Para-alcoholics are reactors rather than actors.

Even if you relate to only a few of these, I find it remarkable how similar the characteristics of dysfunctional people are. And I thought I was so unique! A.A. is a subtle *re-education* process, gently moving me from an unhealthy to a healthy woman if I am willing to follow the path thoroughly.

When I was a newcomer and "encouraged" by my sponsor to attend the women's meeting, I began to learn how to evaluate and appreciate each encounter without expectations or demands. I started learning to be "a friend among friends" without attaching myself like a barnacle. I could safely practice new ideas in A.A. without fear of being kicked out or ridiculed. I had read the Third Tradition! I began to learn what the professionals call "**boundaries**." I have written about boundaries in previous Traditions. Still, it bears repeating because it's such an essential part of emotional sobriety – of being a grown-up.

Establishing "boundaries" is about essential social interaction – knowing what's mine and what's not mine and taking action necessary to protect and take care of *Me* in a healthy way while not overstepping *your* boundaries in the process Healthy boundaries are essential to physical, emotional, and spiritual health. They may be different for each person and each relationship, and boundaries may change over time. Let's break that down:

Physical boundaries are easy to see in the material world – fences, signs, and so on, which state, "This is where my property begins and ends." Knowing what I own gives me freedom. Within the confines of my property, I can plant anything I want – flowers, grass, trees, or nothing at all.

Emotional and *spiritual* boundaries are just as accurate but more challenging to see. Those boundaries define what is me and what is not, what is my responsibility and what is not (spoiler alert: other people are *not* my responsibility unless they are two years old and in diapers!). Knowing my emotional and spiritual boundaries gives me freedom, too.

However, if I do not "own" my life, there is no freedom. If I don't own my own life, I have nothing to contribute to anything or anybody.

A lack of boundaries indicates that I don't have a solid personal identity or that I am entangled with others. A lack of healthy boundaries can negatively affect every aspect of my life. In the past, my only coping skill with my lack of boundaries was to move, to physically withdraw from being engulfed.

When confronted with my lack of ownership of my own life and my need for personal boundaries, I asked these questions:

- What are boundaries?
- What if I upset or hurt someone by my boundaries?
- How do I deal with someone who wants my time, love, energy, or money?
- Why do I feel guilty or afraid about setting boundaries?
- Am I just being selfish by setting boundaries?

My sponsor taught me, "If I do the right thing for me, it will be the right thing for others." It took me a long time to see the wisdom in this principle. It sounded selfish – the root of my troubles. However, the "right thing for me" is to establish and maintain healthy boundaries in my interactions with others. Healthy boundaries are a critical component of self-care. I am responsible for the things that make up "me."

If other people try to make me responsible for their feelings or their lives, that is about them, not me!

What's mine and what's not mine?

When I have no boundaries, I feel resentful, full of self-pity, and overwhelmed. Healthy boundaries can make the difference between a happy relationship and a dysfunctional one.

How do I set personal and emotional boundaries? I must define what I mean by a boundary and what it means to me:

- **Expect respect** – It's a fundamental right.
- **Communicate** – I must say what I need.
- **Don't over-explain** – "No" is a complete sentence.
- **Establish consequences**: I must say why it's important to me, keep the focus on me (there's a world of difference between saying, "I need" and "You have to"), and be willing to follow through if the boundary is violated.

Here are more examples of boundaries:

Physical boundaries: This includes my need for personal space, my comfort with touch, and my physical needs, like needing to rest or have time alone.

Emotional boundaries: This boundary is about honoring feelings and energy – knowing when to share me and when not to share – *limiting* my emotional sharing with people who respond critically or dismissively. And when I respect the emotional boundaries of others, I validate their feelings and energy.

Violations of these emotional boundaries include:

- Dismissing and criticizing feelings.
- Asking questions that are not appropriate for the relationship.
- Asking people to justify their feelings.
- Assuming I know how other people feel.
- Telling other people how *they* feel.

Time Boundaries: I was always "running out of time." Setting time boundaries means understanding my priorities and the time available to include all the areas in my life without over-committing. Organizing the time I give to others is much easier when I establish my priorities.

Time violations include:

- Demanding time from people.
- Showing up late.
- Canceling because I'm overcommitted.

Intellectual boundaries: Healthy intellectual boundaries include respect for the ideas of other people, whether or not they agree with my ideas;

Violations of this intellectual boundary:

- Choosing inappropriate times to begin a potentially disagreeable discussion (at the Thanksgiving dinner table, for example).
- Criticizing or dismissing someone because they have a different opinion.

Material boundaries: This boundary refers to my possessions —home, car, clothing, jewelry, money, etc. It is healthy to understand what I will and will not share and how I expect my "stuff" to be treated by others.

Violations include:

- Destruction of "borrowed" items.
- Borrowing too frequently.
- The use of money or possessions to manipulate or control relationships.

I can't tell you how miserable and guilty I felt when I first began to set boundaries with the people in my life. It took the phrase "willing to go to any length" to a new level! My friend Sandy prays, "Lord, take me to different." I still say that prayer when confronted with my *slumbering codependency*!

With the new awareness of *"what's mine and what's not"* and continuous practice in this area, it became easier to honor myself and others. I make it sound so easy, but the mental anguish is very real when I deliberately begin to act in ways that contradict my old familiar patterns of thinking and behavior. I still remember awkwardly setting a boundary with an A.A. friend, then wanting to run after her, saying, "Wait! I didn't mean it! Let's go back to the old way of doing things!" Of course, I didn't run after her, and I learned that *I can sit still with uncomfortable feelings* and not die! Think about it – how many times have I taken an action, any action, just to get away from my emotions? How childish!

Over time and with repetition, these new patterns of thinking and behavior replace the old, unhealthy habits and become the new normal!

However, if I do not "own" my life, there is no freedom.

It's all about respect. Just as I ask for respect for my separate identity, feelings, and thoughts, I must respect the same thing in others.

There's lots of information about "boundaries" on the internet, and it's easy to access.

When we set boundaries for ourselves, we allow others to understand and respect us. *We teach people how to treat us. Now there is a statement to ponder!* By being a doormat, I'm saying, "It's okay, walk all over me," and they do.

Tradition Seven is about boundaries. It is also about learning how to achieve genuine autonomy (freedom from the bondage of self). Autonomy is also about responsibility. There is no freedom without responsibility, and while A.A. allows us to enjoy a tremendous amount of freedom, it also asks us to carefully guard and maintain our primary purpose., which is to stay sober and carry the message to the alcoholic who still suffers. And for this, each of us is responsible.

So, it makes sense that, as individuals, we can't put ourselves in a position to be indebted to anyone or anything. "Whoever pays the piper calls the tune."

You have probably noticed many similarities between Tradition Six and Tradition Seven. They both concern the healthy need for each person to strive to become their own individual selves without being overly dependent on others for their identification or their very existence.

In earlier Traditions, we've been talking about each partner's responsibility to a group, whether it's a group of two (a marriage), a group of co-workers (a business organization), another group of two (friends), or a group of strangers (in a grocery store or an airport).

There must be a sense of unity and cooperation to be a healthy group, no matter how many members. The individuals involved must be willing to subjugate their self-centered egos to protect the group's integrity, even if that group consists of just two people. Everyone in the group should be autonomous except in matters affecting the group. Courtesy and spirituality go hand-in-hand in fostering group harmony. The "we" is more important than the "you" or the "I." The whole is greater than the sum of its parts. That is synergy.

I have written about the 100% commitment. I have written about the need for a new pair of glasses to replace the old ones, which reflects our sometimes biased beliefs about the right and wrong way to do things, think things, and feel things!

I have written about how new and more effective ideas have successfully replaced defective thinking when we incorporate the Traditions into our daily lives. I have written about the importance of good communication skills and active listening.

Here's the big deal: Tradition Seven is about the individual's responsibility separately and within the partnership or group. This is just a different facet of the thinking we found in Tradition Six. It's also a different aspect of the concept behind "boundaries." It's all about growing up!

Here's a novel idea: to have this kind of healthy responsibility towards *myself*, I must have a healthy *"self-centeredness."* I know this sounds like a contradiction to our primary problem of self-*centeredness*. But think about it: to be emotionally sane, I have to be centered inside myself rather than outside of me. When I'm centered outside myself in other people's opinions, in what I think they want me to be for them to like me or to get what I want – I am insane – I am not myself. If I'm not myself, how can I possibly have a healthy relationship with another? Especially if they are not themselves either!

All my life, I had lived with the false belief that other people's opinions of me were more important than *my* opinion of me.

All my life, I thought that to get anywhere in life, I had to impress, control, manipulate, compete with, and, at the same time, get along with everybody in my life!

When I came to A.A., all I heard about was powerlessness, unmanageability, surrender, and acceptance; nothing about gaining control over people, places, and things in my life. What was wrong with you people? Didn't you know what was important in life? Didn't *God* know what was important in life?

I slowly learned a new way of thinking about my old attitude. I came to believe that the more I tried to control someone or something else, the more I was headed toward disaster. This was because my self-esteem depended on whether they did or didn't do whatever I wanted them to do.

When I grasped this concept, I began to understand the phrase "anxious apartness," which is mentioned in the 12 x

12 in Step 5. When I first read it as a newcomer, that phrase hit me like a ton of bricks. As with most things in A.A., when I first saw it, I didn't understand it, but somehow knew it was important, so I wrote it down and filed it away for future contemplation! I had lived my entire life feeling anxious apartness from everything – God, you, and even myself.

I blamed you for this feeling of anxiety and felt powerless to change it. Since *you* caused it, *you* had to change it, and you didn't. I learned in Alcoholics Anonymous that I had been the one who separated; I was creating anxiety. You didn't do that to me; God didn't do that to me. *I* did that to myself. I caused myself a lot of unnecessary grief through the manipulations I performed in an effort to control everything!

Check out pages 60-62 in our Big Book for a complete description!

In A.A., I heard that "Happiness is an inside job." I didn't understand what it meant, but this instinctively hit a nerve in me. It felt right. I began to search for more than *physical* sobriety – I wanted spiritual, mental, and emotional sobriety as well.

My goal became to be comfortable *inside of me* despite whatever was happening or not happening *outside of me*. Step Ten in the 12 x 12 says it best: *"It is a spiritual axiom that every time we are disturbed, no matter what the cause, there is something wrong with us."*

My feelings live inside of me and come *from* me, not from outside people or circumstances. Now, there's a concept I could finally grasp intellectually but had difficulty translating into my daily life.

But what about when someone says ugly things about me to other people? What about when I want to go to the beach, and it rains? There is something wrong with me because I've made a *judgment*. I have an opinion about how people and circumstances ought to be according to me, me, me!

I didn't know it then, but my expectations became demands, and when they were not met, I was crushed with that old feeling of unworthiness. Last Chapter, we discussed Bill Wilson's "Emotional Sobriety" article. Talk about a new pair of glasses! This new attitude goes a long way toward moving me closer to the peace and serenity I had been seeking my whole life. It took a long time before that new attitude reached my heart and became somewhat automatic.

Repetition! Repetition!

For the same reason, I'm not responsible for the feelings of others, either. I thought I was, which gave me a *momentary sense of power*, but I was wrong about that, too!

This is why, when Bill and I were challenged to sit knee to knee, holding hands, saying the Serenity Prayer out loud, and inviting God into our discussion, Tradition Seven made the statement "You make me feel..." a lie!

Tradition Seven says this thinking is also a lie in the outside world. Other people didn't *make me feel* a certain way, and circumstances didn't *make me feel* a certain way (like rain when I wanted to go to the beach). My *thinking* made me feel this way. It was my choice, although I usually didn't think so. My thinking is an inside job as well. I didn't realize how much my thinking determines both the direction and the quality of my life. My thinking talks to me all the time, *incessantly*. Sometimes, it even wakes me up to talk to me in the middle of the night. And by its continuous **bullying**, I have allowed it to control my feelings and my actions. My thinking had influenced my life, and I was unaware of it. I had the cart before the horse. I am responsible for what goes on *inside* of me. My thoughts and other people have only as much influence on me as I give to them.

All this is nice, but let me tell you how I realized this – *by doing many things wrong and staying sober anyway*. I operated under my old system until I realized it didn't work, probably never had, and certainly never would! "Gradually" is an abbreviation for "extreme pain, primarily to the false ego, creating humility and a new set of beliefs!"

And this is all about relationships!

For example, self-supporting becomes impossible if one of the partners is the higher power. The same is true for the overly dependent partner. They are both using each other for their own emotional well-being. Each one cannot feel whole without a partner in their life. This partnership dependency easily translates to a faulty dependence on people, places, and circumstances outside us.

If we cannot be responsible for ourselves individually, we cannot be equal in our relationships – or any relationship in the outside world. Bill and I conceded that neither of us had ever been in an "equal" relationship. Someone was always the boss, someone the underling. We could take either role, depending on the parties involved.

We each had to work with our sponsors, the Traditions, and each other to have an equal voice in our relationship. We also found that we did *much better* when we worked on ourselves rather than each other!

This strengthened our relationship as we each became responsible for our *own* growth and spiritual progress *independent of the other*. Regardless of our feelings, we began to want the best possible growth in the other partner.

One of the great gifts of the Steps and Traditions of Alcoholics Anonymous is knowing what is mine and what is not mine. This is the way to freedom! This is so hard to explain because it is a spiritual awakening, a shift in perspective.

I always assumed that almost everything was mine. Naturally, it was a control thing. I believed I was responsible for you, your feelings, and your behavior. Imagine my surprise when I became aware that almost everything was not mine. My attitude, my feelings, and my behavior are mine; nearly everything else is *not* mine.

Here are some examples: how you feel is not mine, what you say about me is not mine, what the weather does is not mine, how my grown-up child behaves in life is not mine, and traffic is not mine.

Taking responsibility for these things is idiotic, but I spent the first part of my life believing this was true and acting accordingly. I didn't know what was mine and what was not mine.

Let me tell you a story from the pamphlet "Acceptance – the way to serenity and peace of mind." This little booklet is not conference-approved but was given to me as a newcomer. The following story will explain why I treasure its wisdom:

"I thought it was my duty to try to solve other people's problems, arbitrate their disputes, and show them how to live their lives. I was hurt when they rejected my unsolicited advice. I finally learned that you cannot help people unless they need help, are willing to be helped, want you to help them, and *ask you to help* them. Even then, you can only help them to help themselves.

An old Arab, whose tent was pitched next to a company of whirling dervishes, was asked, "When they whirl, don't they bother you?" "No." "What do you do about them?" *"I let them whirl!"*

Isn't that a powerful message? I am *self*-centered if I can learn to let others whirl instead of getting caught up in their stuff. Your drama about your cheating boyfriend or lousy boss is not my drama. I can't be helpful to you if I'm all caught up in your emotions, making them my own. If I'm other-centered, I'm always exhausted as I try to navigate your life as well as my own. I have a friend who says, "If I live my life for others, they have two lives; I have none!"

Slowly, I began to experience other people, places, and things as *separate* from me in a healthy sense, not as extensions of me to be controlled and manipulated. I began to see that **what other people did or said about me was about them, not me**. This is so important. It is the key to serenity and peace of mind. My sponsor told me that what other people said about me was none of my business!

Acceptance is the only real source of tranquility. In his story "Acceptance is the Answer," in the Fourth Edition of the Big Book, Dr. Paul says, "Acceptance is the answer to all my problems today. When I am disturbed, it is because I find some person, place, thing, or situation – some fact of my life – unacceptable to me, and I can find no serenity until I accept that person, place, thing, or situation as being exactly the way it is supposed to be at this moment. *Nothing, absolutely nothing, happens in God's world by mistake.* Until I could accept my alcoholism, I could not stay sober; unless I accept life entirely on life's terms, I cannot be happy. I need to concentrate not so much on what needs to be changed in the world but on what needs to be changed in me and *my attitudes.*"

I'm writing this after many years of trial and error and practice, practice, practice! In sobriety, I am learning to change my behavior to something more favorable to harmony. As a direct result of this perseverance, I've found a place of peace. In the deepest part of me, I've found joy and serenity. It is where my God lives. I call it the "NOW." (the Big Book says: "There is one who has all power, that one is God. May you find him NOW").

If I leave this place of "NOW" to go into the past or future, I go alone because God always stays in the "NOW." I have *fearful* feelings if I'm alone in the future. If I'm in the past, alone, I have *remorseful* or *resentful* feelings. Unless I do my umpteenth Fourth Step, these negative feelings will not add to the peace and serenity I seek. So, I try to keep my thinking and feeling confined to that little room inside me called "the NOW." This allows God to work in my life instead of me orchestrating the show.

When I choose to do this, practicing the Steps and Traditions in my daily life is so much easier.

Everything is always all right *in this moment*. I can let go and let God *in the moment*. I can practice love and tolerance of others *for the moment*. I can legitimately achieve (moment to moment) my primary purpose for being on this earth: "to fit myself to be of maximum service to God and those about me." *In the moment*, I can be useful, happy, joyous, and free.

Life is all about relationships. Tradition Seven is about responsibly choosing, maintaining, and supporting my relationships spiritually, emotionally, and physically in a healthy fashion.

And isn't that what it's all about?

Chapter Seven

Questions from Tradition Seven

1. *Is my self-esteem based inside rather than outside of me? (in other people's opinions, the need for approval, etc.)*

2. *Am I dependent on others for my emotional well-being? (Can another person's anger or disapproval ruin my whole day?)*

3. *Do I blame others for how I feel? Why?*

4. *Am I the higher power for the other person in the relationship? (partner, people I sponsor, grown children, etc.?)*

5. *Do I understand that when I try to control others, I give them control? Explain.*

6. *Do I have to have a romantic relationship to feel whole? Why?*

7. *Do I believe I am responsible for my physical, emotional, and spiritual maintenance and growth? If not, why not?*

8. *Do I suffer from a feeling of "anxious apartness"? What does that mean to me?*

9. *Do I take responsibility for my feelings or blame others for them?*

10. *Do I generate my feelings from within me? Why? If not, why not?*

11. *Do I believe that I am responsible for the feelings of others? Why? If not, why not?*

12. *Do I believe that acceptance of life on life's terms is the answer? (Read the story "**Acceptance was the Answer**" in the 4th edition of the book, Alcoholics Anonymous.)*

13. *Do I try to live in the moment, in the "NOW"? Why?*

14. *Am I an equal in my relationships? Do I walk shoulder to shoulder with others?*

15. *Am I willing to make changes in myself in order to have healthy relationships? If not, why not? How will I begin?*

16. *Have I suffered from addictions in my life **before** my alcohol addiction? Describe these addictions. (For example, reading, eating, exercising, spending, gambling).*

17. *Have I suffered from addictions in my life **after** coming into Alcoholics Anonymous? Describe these addictions.*

Specific Tasks Matter!

IN THE 12 X 12, the Eighth Tradition states: "Alcoholics Anonymous should remain forever nonprofessional, but our service centers may employ special workers."

For our purposes, the Eighth Tradition could say that marriage (or any relationship) should forever be free, giving, and reciprocal. Still, each *group* may *mutually* agree upon specific tasks and responsibilities for each person in the group.

Tradition Eight emphasizes the importance of *equality* and the avoidance of hierarchy in *any* relationship. I have written about this in other Traditions: the need for mutual respect and shared decision-making between partners. Tradition Eight implies that a healthy relationship will grow when both contribute as equals according to the qualities and strengths each brings to the relationship. *I've heard that you have one partner too many if both partners are exactly alike!* Bill and I had to learn to appreciate each other's *individuality*, skills, and unique contributions to our relationship.

What a wonderful concept. If only it were that simple!

It began with a hesitant acceptance of my individuality and separateness and Bill's individuality and separateness. When we married, and the battle for power and control began, he and I spent lots of time with our sponsors trying to sort things out. We thought we could return to our idyllic, impractical courtship, where everything was "perfect." That never happened, of course. But here's what **did** happen: one morning, I admitted to my sponsor, *"Maybe I'm a little bit at fault in this mess."* What a turning point! This was a necessary ego deflation and an acknowledgment that while Bill and I were a *group* of two, Bill and I were separate individuals. I began to examine "the exact nature of *my* wrongs."

I discovered that I lacked a sense of responsibility for myself – I had always believed that others were the source of my happiness or unhappiness, and I was *always* disappointed. I exemplified what Bill Wilson wrote about in 1958 in his letter on *emotional sobriety*: "I was overly dependent on other people to supply me with prestige, security, and the like. I had fought for them, failing to get them according to my perfectionist dreams. *My dependency meant demand* – a demand for the possession and control of the people and conditions surrounding me."

I depended on *my* Bill to provide me with perfect, peaceful love; instead, he was constantly arguing with me and trying to control me! I had a hole inside and demanded he fill it, but I was so self-absorbed that I couldn't see *he* had the same emptiness. I was so busy trying to get him to love me as I demanded that I had no strength left to love him. *There was no reciprocity.*

Reciprocity means a mutual exchange – "The agreements or policies in dealings between people in which corresponding advantages or privileges are granted by each to the other." A mutual exchange. It is, by definition, a two-way street. We had no reciprocity. We were two sick puppies.

But we had each made that 100% commitment to our marriage. We both knew that a promise is nothing without action. **If faith without works is dead,** *insight* *without action is fantasy*. We had to learn how to listen to each other, how to communicate with each other, how to empathize (that means stepping into each other's shoes), and most importantly, how to gain total *acceptance* of the other person at this moment in time, knowing that person will change. Thomas Merton writes, "The *beginning* of love is to let those we love be perfectly themselves, and not twist them to fit our image, otherwise we love only the reflection of *ourselves* we find in them."

We will *all* change. It's our decision *how* we change. We will grow spiritually, or we will not. In our spiritual life, we drift backward unless we move forward.

I can't believe it, but I've spent almost half a century pondering, seeking, and practicing the A.A. Blueprint for Living. To find serenity, I had to decide a thousand times to relinquish the need for **control**, the need for **approval**, and the need to **judge**. Then I had to take the actions that the decision required. This is not an overnight matter. I became impatient when my sponsor said, "*Give time, time.*" It is an *event* at a time, many *days* at a time, sometimes *minutes* at a time, discovering, confronting, and becoming *willing* to let go of my old attitudes and beliefs in the face of the realities of sobriety. I know for a fact that I'm not a finished product yet!

When I got to A.A., I knew there was more wrong with me than *drinking*. I wanted to "fix" what was wrong with me. I had tried being just "undrunk" (another term for untreated alcoholism) by stopping drinking. It was awful.

You know how I felt if you have gone a few days, weeks, or even months denying yourselves the *relief* of that first drink. I was restless, irritable, and resentful. Everything annoyed me, including *me!* When I finally took that first drink, it relieved the pain and distress of what I called "reality." I could breathe again.

That being said, when I finally found A.A., I had already surrendered to the greater power of alcohol. One day prior to A.A., while pouring my first drink of the morning, I had the soul-sickening realization that my scotch bottle *owned* me, and I was powerless over its demands. I had turned my life and will over to that bottle.

When I "*officially*" surrendered to this powerlessness, I hesitantly became willing to believe that there is *another* Power greater than alcohol ...*or me!* I came to believe that Power is everything, and for lack of a better word, I call that Power "God." I became willing to proceed using that Power as a guide. I also came to believe that another name for this Power is "*unconditional love.*" **Love and tolerance of others is our code.** This is one of the most profound sentences in our Big Book. Because I came to believe that he created me and lives in me, I came to believe that he created *you* and lives in *you* as well. This would mean that we each have the same spiritual potential.

"*Namaste*," a concept I first heard in yoga, means "The spirit in me recognizes and *salutes* the spirit in you." A.A. has taught me that belief is nothing unless accompanied by action. Faith without works is dead, and insight without action is fantasy. When I first got sober, the only thing I could cling to (aside from my sponsor) was the Serenity Prayer. I instinctively knew that the action in the Serenity Prayer was to accept or change. I must accept a situation or change my attitude.

I've told you that one of the greatest gifts I've gotten in A.A. is knowing what is mine and what is not. 99% of what I must **accept** is *outside* of me (not mine), and 99% of what I must **change** is *inside* me (mine). And how do I do this? ***Through my changed actions, my thoughts and feelings change***. My friend Sandy prays, "*God, take me to different*." Before I found A.A., if I had an agenda – a situation where I wanted something from you, I would try the tactics described so *powerfully* on pages 60-62 of our Big Book: "We are like an actor who wants to run the whole show; is forever trying to arrange the lights, the ballet, the scenery and the rest of the players in his own way. In trying to make these arrangements, our actor may sometimes be quite virtuous. He may be kind, considerate, patient, generous, even modest, and self-sacrificing. On the other hand, he may be mean, egotistical, selfish, and dishonest. What usually happens? The show doesn't come off very well. He decides to exert himself more."

I was indeed self-will run riot! This is the mindset of the woman who was trying to have a healthy relationship with a man who had the same warped perspective.

Let's go back to the beginning of my sobriety: I first began to *experience* "unconditional love," this God in me recognizing and saluting the God in you, when I was three weeks sober and started going on Twelve-Step calls with my sponsor. A Twelve-Step call is where a person calls the A.A. office asking for help with a drinking problem.

Two members of A.A. go out and share with that person about themselves *and* Alcoholics Anonymous. When my sponsor and I completed a Twelve-Step call, a feeling came over me I had never felt before: I truly wanted the best for these women without wanting or needing anything in return. In the past, I had a mental scorecard in every relationship. On this scorecard, I kept a list of my expectations and demands for reciprocal payback if I did anything for you. There was always a price to be paid.

I didn't feel this way on those Twelve-Step calls. I felt love flowing **out** of me for the first time ever! Of course, I spent fruitless hours afterward analyzing this amazing phenomenon. It's funny, but when I try to "figure something out," I'm really saying, "When I understand this, I can control it." I did this a lot about drinking. I just wanted to "get a handle on it " to continue drinking without negative consequences. In early sobriety, I was *way* too self-absorbed to see that my sponsor gave me unconditional love. She *accepted* me just as I was at that moment. She met me where *I* was, knowing that I could not meet her where *she* was. She was unfailingly courteous and loving to me in every encounter. I shudder now to think how callously I treated the time and effort she put into our relationship.

When I was about *three years sober*, the following incident took place that illustrates my arrogant and self-centered orientation: We met every Thursday during her lunch break (Tommie worked as a counselor at the only detox/treatment center in Ft. Lauderdale at that time). One day, she drove up to "our" restaurant, rolled down the window, and told me we couldn't meet because she was *sick* and going home. We had no cell phones back then, so Tommie could have either not shown up or come to the restaurant to tell me in person. Tommie drove to the restaurant. On *my* drive home, I was *furious*. I fumed, "How dare she make me come all this way for nothing? Doesn't she know how busy I am (I wasn't!) and that I could have made better use of my valuable time? (I couldn't!) I'll show her; I'll get another sponsor who *appreciates* me!" Thank God I didn't follow through, and for many years, I never told Tommie that she had been briefly fired!

Isn't that a great example of *self-obsession*? Self-centeredness? The world revolved around me, me, me. Where was the unconditional love or even *empathy* on my part?

This was pretty much my attitude when I met Bill and three years later married him. I had no idea of the unrealistic self-oriented expectations I placed on myself, Bill, and our relationship, but I found out almost immediately after we married. I started describing him as "That selfish man. *After all I've done for him.* He should at least do this for me. He owes me!" My scorecard was alive and well. I'm sure he had his own tally sheet and was keeping *his* scores! We didn't know this came from our judgmental, critical, and controlling natures. *Each of us was right in our own minds!*

Dating expectations and **married** expectations are different. For some reason, while we're dating, we think that *if* we get married, the relationship will

- Stay the same,
- Magically get better,

- *He* will change for the better because of *her*,
- Because of him, she will *never* change from the perfection she is now (adoring, sexy, and always physically perfect).

Guess what, folks? None of the above is true!

Since we never resolved any conflict or disagreement we experienced while dating, the issues *tripled* in size and intensity when we married. Now, we live in the same house and cannot take a break from each other as we could before we were married and lived in two separate places.

I've told you some of our journey, together and separately, into **emotional sobriety**. I've told you how it took time, two loving sponsors, and our respective loving higher powers to restore us to sanity on the road to a loving, healthy, *grown-up* relationship.

We discovered how important Alcoholics Anonymous was to our *perception* and our *marriage*. Bill took a business trip to Canada right after we were married, and I went with him. Sort of a honeymoon, we thought. We did not seek out A.A. meetings as we always had in the past when we traveled. We stuck to ourselves and were ready to file for divorce by the time we got home. We came home on Sunday and couldn't call a lawyer until Monday, so we went to an

A.A. meeting. We could have chosen to stay home and argue – how spiritual is that? But *as* we walked in the door to that meeting, something happened for *both* of us. We looked at each other and smiled. We were home again, and everything was right again. A.A. is definitely an attitude adjuster!

This incident showed me that I live in two realities simultaneously. One reality is inside my head in my *thoughts* and *feelings*. The other reality is the outside world and is made up of my **actions**. I manifest my spirituality through my actions. ***I manifest my spirituality through my actions.***

All my good intentions and loving thoughts in my inner reality (my head) have no meaning unless translated into external reality as caring, thoughtful acts. ***My*** thinking ***defines my reality unless challenged by my actions.***

Bill and I took the *spiritual action* of attending an A.A. meeting, and our *thinking* and *feelings* changed. We took the healthy *action* and got the healthy *results*.

We stand at a turning point many times each day. The *choices* we make determine the *quality* of our lives. Self-centeredness slips away when we live by the Principles of the Twelve Steps and the Twelve Traditions. By "slips away," I mean we're like the duck floating serenely in the lake – underwater, his feet paddle like crazy! And that's what we do. That's what Bill and I did that night – we "worked" the program of Alcoholics Anonymous. *"Nothing changed, but everything was different."*

Here's a great example of Bill's loving attitude and behavior: Bill was a private pilot – he had learned how to fly in the Air Force – and we enjoyed flying together. Sometimes, we would fly from Ft. Lauderdale to Key West, Florida, on a Sunday morning to attend an A.A. meeting at their beautiful new Clubhouse, have lunch with some of the members there, and then fly home. As a passenger, I was thrilled to watch the landscape go by from thousands of feet in the air. I decided to take flying lessons after hearing on the news one morning of this harrowing incident: a man flying a small plane had a heart attack, and his wife had to land the plane. She did not know how to fly. Fortunately, she did know how to operate the radio, and she was safely talked down out of the sky by a pilot on the ground. After listening to this incredible tale, I trotted myself over to our local airport and began taking landing lessons. Did you know there's a course available to learn how to land an airplane?

Of course, that wasn't enough for *this* alcoholic who suffers from the disease of *"more."* I absolutely fell in love with flying and became a private pilot.

I never knew till years later that Bill had been full of fear for me every time I would go flying alone, perfecting my skills. He later told me that every time I left for the airport, he wanted to ask me to stop flying because of *his* fear. He never voiced his concerns because he knew it would potentially affect my self-esteem and growth. The unspoken message behind his fear was that I was inadequate and could only fail.

Once again, it was a control issue. Together, we had made the decision to go to any lengths to achieve a true partnership. Bill realized that *his* thoughts and feelings about me and the dangers of flying were *his* thoughts and feelings, having nothing to do with me.

Of course, if he had voiced those fears, it was my responsibility to decide how I felt about flying and my ability to do so. I could no longer live by the self-centered philosophy of being my own boss and doing only what *I* wanted to do.

We wanted to be a partnership of equals, and we gradually, most times painfully, grew to *be* those equal partners.

One of the hardest lessons Bill and I had to learn was how to *confront* each other *lovingly*. The only way *I* knew how to talk about differences was to accuse, blame, accuse, blame – usually in a very loud voice. The flip side of this was shoving it under the rug, hoping the lump in the carpet would trip him. Resentment comes in many silly forms.

I learned that *loving* confrontation is sometimes necessary to encourage spiritual growth. I shared a lot about this when I wrote in earlier Traditions about "Fair Fighting," "Active Listening," and "Communication skills."

Loving confrontation is part of what makes up **any** meaningful relationship. This is also true of all *friendships* which have substance and depth and is **essential** in the area of *sponsorship*. This *learned* skill to confront lovingly is certainly true when sponsoring. Despite my selfish attitude toward Tommie (and everyone else on the planet) early in sobriety, I began to *learn* how to be a good sponsor through the gradual changes brought about *in me* through the Steps and Traditions.

I studied the Chapter "Working with Others" in our Big Book. I read and reread the A.A. pamphlet on sponsorship. I talked to my sponsor about sponsoring, and I sponsored. Even though I did my best to follow the guidelines I was given, I still made *lots* of mistakes. I didn't drink alcohol in the process, so I was a successful sponsor.

I loved hearing Tommie tell the story of being at the General Service Office in New York and talking with Bill Wilson. She was complaining about the women she sponsored who weren't staying sober. "Tommie," Bill said, "Do you think I sponsored Dr. Bob so *he* would stay sober?" "Of course," Tommie said. *"No," said Bill. "I sponsored Dr. Bob so* **I** *would stay sober!"*

There's an important distinction here! As a result, I made a 180-degree turn in my attitude toward sponsorship. ***I sponsor so I will stay sober.*** I have to give away what I learn in order to keep it. At seven years of sobriety, this insight changed everything about how I defined sponsorship. I realized that my ***only*** responsibility is to share with another alcoholic what was shared with me through our literature and our program of recovery: how to *"expel the obsession to drink and enable the sufferer to become happily and usefully whole."*

I finally learned about "GIVING." *It's an attitude.* The dictionary defines it this way: "To present voluntarily without expecting compensation," "to place in someone's care," "to offer." This is a beautiful definition of sponsorship as well as every other relationship. Of course, this giving must be accomplished within healthy boundaries, as we previously discussed in earlier Traditions. Giving is not being a doormat; it's an *attitude*. It's an attitude of *self-respect* and *respect for others*. I believe I first experienced this purity while on the Twelve-Step calls I made with my sponsor when I was three weeks sober.

I loved these women. I also began to love any woman *newer* than I was in the program. I *gave* them my time and attention. I treated them with courtesy and respect. I shared my experience, strength, and hope with them. I made them feel important because they *were* important. I expected nothing in return, and *I* was staying sober! Then I experienced *another* miracle when I saw the newcomer *I* had treated with love and respect treating a *newer* newcomer with the same love and respect.

This is generational giving. This is giving at its finest. This is true joy.

By the way, I also began to understand *my* sponsor's attitude towards *me* throughout the ups and downs of my sobriety. It also softened the guilt of my early, self-centered behavior toward *her* when I experienced the same self-centered behavior from the women *I* was sponsoring. Nothing personal, just early sobriety – and sometimes *not* so early!

Gradually, I expanded my free, giving, and reciprocal attitude toward other people in the A.A. program and those with whom I came into contact who were *not* in A.A. This included my neighbor, the clerk at the grocery store, and the acquaintance at the gym where I worked out—the ripple effect.

It's funny, but the last people to come onto my "giving" radar were those closest to me: my sponsor, my father, my daughter, my best friend, and ultimately, Bill. I think that's because a momentary "giving" commitment at the grocery store doesn't involve much effort and certainly not a long-term commitment. The closer the relationship, the heavier the commitment with a capital "C." But even *these* relationships began to change as I sought to become more spiritually fit through my actions.

Let's go back to sponsorship for a minute. It's funny, but I have to be in good spiritual condition to sponsor, and I will become in good spiritual condition by sponsoring! I learned to detach emotionally from their problems. When a woman I sponsor feels terrible about something, I will understand and support her *sobriety*. But I'm not responsible for her *feelings*. I don't have to *participate* in her feelings – most assuredly, I don't have to "fix" her feelings with all my good, unsolicited advice – by the way, *unsolicited advice is always criticism!* This is true in any relationship.

I once created a **"Sponsorship Contract."** On one side of the paper, I wrote, "What I Am Willing To Do As Your Sponsor." I then listed such things as "I will guide you through the Twelve Steps and Twelve Traditions of Alcoholics Anonymous." "I will never do for you what you can do for yourself." "I will help you develop a program for living and working with the God of *your* understanding – not mine." I added, "I will never talk about you or divulge anything we've discussed." And "I will never ask you to do something I'm not doing myself or am unwilling to do."

On the other side of the sheet of paper, I made a list entitled: "What I Require From You" (the woman being sponsored). "You will regularly attend A.A. meetings." "You will have regular contact with me – eyeball to eyeball at least once a week outside of meetings *if possible*." "You will read and study the Big Book of Alcoholics Anonymous and attend a Big Book study group *if possible*." "You will join a home group and be active in it – go early, stay late, help with setting up, cleaning up, making coffee." "You will attend group conscience meetings in your home group."

Here's probably the most crucial aspect of sponsorship I included: "It is *your* responsibility to tell me what is happening with you; *I am not a mind reader*." How many times have I heard a woman I sponsor say, "Yes, something big happened in my life yesterday or two weeks ago, but I didn't want to bother you. I know how busy you are." I've done this myself, and later saw the self-defeating, judgmental position I was taking. I was deciding for her how busy she was and deciding my life wasn't important enough to "bother" her. Talk about hanging onto "old ideas!"

I added a few other things to personalize the contract for each woman. The idea of the contract was to clearly understand each party's obligations in the relationship. This is Tradition Eight in action: "We had mutually agreed upon specific tasks and responsibilities for each person in the group." My message was, "I'm responsible for sharing the A.A. program (as outlined in our literature) with you. You are responsible for your sobriety and incorporating the A.A. program in your life."

I never said she had to stay sober, although that was our agreed-upon goal. I've never fired anyone because she drank (that would be just exercising one of my control issues, I believe). *It would be more about me than her.* Women have wandered away from me and chosen other sponsors over the years. I wish them well and applaud their need to take care of their own recovery. I believe there is an element of *mutual chemistry* in a sponsorship relationship. We can't be all things to all people. *I'm* the one who has benefitted the most from sponsorship. I've learned to listen to what I say to the women I sponsor because *I* always need to hear it. For example, I may be talking about the 11th Step and listening to myself telling her how important prayer and meditation are in my life. I know I must do my *own* checklist when I hear myself saying those words. Have I been slacking off because I'm too busy? Am I thinking of something else with one channel of my mind when I'm supposedly "meditating?"

Somehow, it seems easier to learn about me through sponsorship than through marriage – I wasn't quite as *defensive* as a sponsor as I was as a wife. Maybe the *permanence* of marriage had me on guard and alert at all times, where sponsorship is based on a potentially brief relationship – each party is always free to move on. With my protective guard down, I can see myself as I am rather than as my ego would have me be.

And so on and so on. I can grow spiritually when I turn the spotlight on myself instead of the other person.

I could go on forever about marriage, sponsorship, and other encounters, illustrating that *any* relationship must be free, giving, and reciprocal to be healthy. It is a concept that was contrary to *everything* I learned growing up, and it took a lot of courage, patience, and practice to change my attitude from "gimmee" to "give."

Bill and I learned that being free, giving, and reciprocal was possible, but who would take out the trash? Who was going to balance the checkbook and pay the bills? Who was responsible for emptying the dishwasher? *While* we were learning how to *listen* to each other and how to *communicate* effectively, we would sit, knee to knee, holding hands, and discuss those issues. We would make decisions and allocate the chores of daily living. What a *difference* from the old self-defeating *power* struggles of our early marriage! We actually *solved* life's little problems without having World War III in our living room.

He took out the trash. How spiritual is that?

Chapter Eight

Questions from Tradition Eight

1. *Is my marriage (or any relationship) a free, giving, and reciprocal relationship?*

   Free _____. What does this mean to me?

   Giving _____. What does this mean to me?

   Reciprocal _____. What does this mean to me?

2. *Does my identity and feelings of self-worth depend on my participation in a relationship?*

3. *Who were my role models for how to be a grown-up man or woman? Were they healthy ones?*

4. *Who were my role models for a good marriage? Were they healthy ones?*

5. *Do I have relationships for fun and free without expecting anything in return? Name two.*

6. *Do I keep a mental scorecard of expectations and demands for payback from others?*

7. *How do I feel about myself when I keep score?*

8. *Do I feel the other person belongs to me (husband, wife, person I sponsor?) Am I possessive of others?*

9. *Do I acknowledge that even though I'm part of a group of two or more, each person in that group is a separate individual?*

10. *Do I accept other people **as** they are and **where** they are? Can I meet them where **they** are without criticism or annoyance that they can't be where **I** am?*

11. *Am I committed to my relationships even when momentarily, the "love" is gone?*

12. *Do I believe that "insight without action is fantasy"? What does that mean to me?*

13. *Have I learned how to lovingly confront my partner, my friend, my grown children, and my co-workers when necessary?*

14. *Do I sponsor so **I** will stay sober or get the **other** person sober?*

15. *What is **my** responsibility to those I sponsor?*

16. *What do I require of those I sponsor?*

17. *Do I need the approval of another to validate me as a person?*

18. *Do I examine my motives to make sure there are no strings attached when doing something for others?*

19. *Have I developed a "giving" attitude towards everyone in my life, no matter how fleeting or long-term?*

20. *Why is my relationship with a God of **my** understanding important in the practice of this Tradition and my life?*

21. *Do I ever ask God to allow **me** to see my partner (or any other person) as **God** sees them?*

Flexible Matters!

In the Twelve and Twelve, the Ninth Tradition reads: "A.A. as such ought never to be organized, but we may create service boards or committees directly responsible to those they serve."

For our purposes of examining and incorporating the Traditions into **our** daily relationships, the Ninth Tradition could read: "A family or any relationship should be *flexible* in its organization; each member is directly responsible to those they serve. Our group conscience may appoint certain persons responsible for serving various functions. Our primary goal is to be of maximum service to God and those about us."

Lofty goals! The Ninth Tradition is all about service – maximum service! It's all about unity. It's all about love.

The Ninth Tradition says the group members are "Directly responsible to those they serve." Who do they serve? *Why, each other, of course.* This is an attitude – a way of connecting to the world. It's an attitude contrary to everything I learned as I grew up. In the beginning, it felt humiliating rather than humbling. There's a saying that we come into A.A. as egomaniacs and work our way up to servants. It's all about the *illusion* of control.

What?

Think about it. Have you ever seen a person less likely to take orders than an alcoholic, drinking or sober? We're like two-year-olds or teenagers, declaring, "Don't tell *me* what to do!"

As newcomers, we don't see that this defiantly self-reliant attitude has been our downfall because *we reject everything but our own ideas* about life and how to live it.

Problems arise because at least two people are involved in every relationship, no matter how fleeting.

Each of us has automatic, unspoken, and largely unconscious roles we've been taught are "right" and which we bring to *every* relationship.

When I was in college, I took many literature courses. One of them taught me the concept of "weltanschauung." This means my "worldview," my *doctrine of beliefs and principles*.

Big word for "*who is supposed to take out the trash* !"

Conflict comes when the people in the relationship have different beliefs, assumptions, and ways of viewing the world. They either are unaware of them or refuse to examine them for **current** validity.

My worldview *drives* me. It determines what I bring to every relationship.

Here's the problem: I will reject it as wrong if your weltanschauung doesn't fit in with my weltanschauung. This isn't because I'm *unreasonable;* it's because I'm *lazy*. It takes *work* to think, maybe even to *re*-think, my assumptions based on life-long observations, experiences, and conclusions. So, my brain, my "***thinker***," rejects your ideas.

In sobriety, it seems that I spend most of my time **gaining** knowledge about myself and my unconscious old ideas about *everything* and then **discarding** *everything*!

Chuck C. describes Alcoholics Anonymous as an Uncovering, Discovering, and Discarding process.

I have been talking about my experience of growing up in A.A. *only as an example* of what we all go through to become partnership-material or relationship-worthy. Believe me; this really *is* about our personal Tradition Nine!

I remember my horror when I began to work on my *second* 4th Step with my Sponsor. Before I talk about *that*, however, let me tell you about my *first* 4th Step:

Remember, my favorite definition of an addiction is: *"A distraction from intolerable reality."* The "intolerable reality" can be what's happening *inside* us, having nothing to do with our outside circumstances. It's about how I feel about myself in relation to the world and the people in it.

I was seven months sober when I wrote my *first* 4th Step – on my own, without any help from my sponsor. I insisted I didn't need her help. I wrote a list of everything wrong I had *ever* done– a list of wretched *behaviors* of which I was ashamed. The *discrepancy* between the "secret Rena" and the "socially acceptable Rena" that I presented to the world was the essence of the **"intolerable reality"** that fueled my addiction. I used addictions, including alcohol, to distract me from acknowledging the intolerable reality about **me.** The truth was that I couldn't bear to face the person I believed I was. Deep down, I defined myself as "bad" and judged myself harshly. Never before had I faced the reality of my beliefs about myself. I was indeed the woman I drank to get away from.

Let me explain: even though my list of "bad" behaviors had *nothing* to do with the *intent* of the 4th step, it served a unique and essential purpose. While confessing everything on my list to my sponsor, she shared with me some of the *same* behaviors she had been ashamed of in *her* life. It was the beginning of the end of isolation for me. I began to see past that mysterious barrier I had always felt between you and me, which I could neither understand nor overcome. I started to believe I could be forgiven and that I could forgive. That *"anxious apartness"* began to dissolve. I inched closer to joining humanity because I took a risk and shared who I believed I was with another human being.

So, when I began to work on a "Big Book" 4th step **with** my sponsor, I found I was looking at the *inside* of me, not the outside *behaviors*. I examined my *character* and some of my character flaws. I discovered some defects that were *not* flattering – I took these appalling items to Tommie in despair. She looked at the list and said, "These defects have all been weapons of defense that made you feel safe as a child. They have been there all along, Rena. In sobriety, you have found they are no longer useful. The only thing that's changed is your *awareness* of them. Now that you're aware, change can happen." I have since come to believe this **awareness** is the beginning of *wisdom*. Awareness has the possibility of bringing about vulnerability, a chink in the defensive wall I'd built up over the years to avoid looking at myself. My core belief, what I *subconsciously* told myself, was that I was a worthless fraud. To *counteract* this belief, I had to be perfect and make my life everyone else's fault. If *you* were responsible, my failures were *your* fault, not mine. No wonder I embraced addictions as distractions from those intolerable and confusing beliefs!

Of course, at the beginning of my sobriety, I was unaware of this harsh self-judgment. I began to trust my sponsor, Alcoholics Anonymous, and God, **in that order**,

I hesitantly and uncomfortably began to open up to seeing things from a new vantage point, to look at life from an *entirely different angle*.

In **my** courtroom, this *always* involved a symbolic walk from the *prosecution* table to the *defense* table. How painful is that? How I did **not** want to do it!

One of my favorite poets, Anais Nin, puts it this way:

"And the day came when the risk to remain tight in a bud was more painful than the risk it took to blossom."

The pain of remaining the same outweighed the pain of change.

Where was I at fault? What was my mistake? What could I have done differently? Once I became aware of the character defects that plagued me, that honest Fourth column became a gateway to freedom – freedom from the bondage of self.

I had completed several Fourth steps with Tommie by the time Bill and I were married. A good thing, too – I needed those *experiences* of looking at myself as honestly as I could in order to face the challenge of viewing myself as a marriage partner.

My first attempts at self-examination were shallow and generic. I believe in that peeling of the onion thing. I *had* to start shallow to dig deeper. Those old ideas that housed my character – my character assets and defects – were peeled away and exposed gently when I was spiritually fit enough to acknowledge and accommodate them. Within a few months of becoming my sponsor, Tommie could have given me a list of everything about my character, useful and not-so-useful, and I would *not* have understood most of it. I would understand the *words,* of course, but not be able to apply them to *me* in any meaningful way. I had to gain some spiritual awareness and spiritual strength before I could recognize who and what I was in order to try to become what *God* would have me *be.*

As a result of this good orderly direction of spiritual growth, by the time Bill and I married and retreated deep into self-centeredness, I was able to climb out of it just enough, with my sponsor's help, to be willing to look at not only *my* old ideas but *Bill's* old ideas as well.

Initially, our sponsors were present when we discussed the right and wrong ways to do things. One of our sponsors might ask, "Who taught you this?" And the other would ask, "Is this true for you today?" Or, "Is this something you want to continue to practice as an adult today?"

A *reasonably* calm discussion would follow, and a decision would be made regarding its validity. On a **good** day, we would have a shiny, brand-new idea for our new and still shiny partnership!

Let's go back to talking about being *"vulnerable, "* an essential aspect of sobriety and relationships.

A synonym for "vulnerable" is "open to attack." I feel exposed and susceptible to being wounded or hurt. It's risky to become *appropriately* vulnerable to our partner, friend, neighbor, co-worker, or clerk in the grocery store.

Another definition of "vulnerable" is "accessible." I like to think of it as "authentic" or "real." Once again, appropriate boundaries are necessary for *healthy* vulnerability, and it took me a long time to achieve a balance. I was either entirely open for everybody or completely shut down and not accessible to anyone. Since I had **no** appropriate boundaries when I came to A.A., I preferred the definition "open to attack" and felt that **no** exposure was better than being hurt. But as the poet said, "The day came when the risk to remain tight in a bud was more painful than the risk it took to blossom." If I become *willing* to keep an open mind and an open heart and *listen* to another person, if I learn who **they** are and what **their** *weltanschauung* is, I can break out of the self-imposed prison of "I know" to acknowledge that "I don't know."

Early in our marriage, Bill and I spent a lot of time trying to understand each other's worldview. It seemed to take *forever* to accept that he had the right to his belief system, just as I had the right to mine. The familiar had a false sense of security, whereas the unknown territory of change was scary. It took *courage* to search for common ground upon which we could agree.

Change takes courage and recovery takes courage because recovery *is* change. It took a lot of courage to walk into my first A.A. meeting. It took courage to ask a woman to be my sponsor and to call that sponsor on the phone. My biggest fear was that I'd say, "This is Rena," and she would say, "Rena, who?" That didn't happen, of course.

It takes courage to try some of the "suggestions" my sponsor made, which involve a behavioral change, especially while I'm still holding onto the **old** fears **of rejection, ridicule, and confrontation.**

I've never changed because someone told me I had to, needed to, or should. It only felt *safe* to change when I felt *accepted* as I am and where I am **right now. A.A. creates an atmosphere of safety and acceptance that makes change possible.** I knew I could make mistakes, and nobody would tell me to leave and never come back. I felt safe practicing new ways of behavior in the rooms of Alcoholics Anonymous. I had never felt that way anywhere else. In the past, the only time I had felt safe was when I was alone.

A good sponsor encourages this kind of acceptance – after all, she's been where I am and knows I will change just as she has changed – *in time.*

In a healthy relationship, the well-being of one is connected to the well-being of all. All flourishing is mutual. We are bound by a covenant of reciprocity, a pact of shared responsibility. My friend Kathy says, "You *can't compete with me; I want you to win, too.*"

"Life on life's terms "is another way of saying "**acceptance.**" *Acceptance is not an event; it is a process.* I can't just get up in the morning, put on my acceptance suit, and be good to go. Acceptance of God's Will for me when I'm home alone saying my pious prayers is not the same as acceptance of God's Will at three in the afternoon when I'm late for an appointment and stuck in traffic! *Every* situation throughout the day requires an *evaluation* of whether I accept it or not.

I believe that *every* time I walk into an A.A. meeting, I am unconsciously practicing acceptance. I'm accepting the first three Steps. I'm surrendering to my powerlessness, getting a sane perspective, and accepting God's Will for me. If I don't continually renew this acceptance of my powerlessness, I may relapse into drinking.

Acceptance is a process, not an event. You'll notice that "*approval*" is not mentioned. I'll never forget the moment I realized I didn't have to *approve* of something to accept it. I thought I did!

By the way, I want to discuss a problem with a "slogan" that surfaced a few years ago: *"Meeting makers make it."* Going to meetings is a foundational step, but why do we attend? Fellowship, of course. Identification as an alcoholic, of course. But we go to meetings to learn about the *program* of Alcoholics Anonymous and how to incorporate that program into our lives so that we can be transformed; transformed from *self*-centeredness to *other*-centeredness through a spiritual awakening. And how does this transformation take place? Through the *program* of A.A.

What does that mean?

The dictionary defines *"program"* as "a plan of action to accomplish a specified end." The *program* **is** the Twelve Steps and Twelve Traditions (and the Twelve Concepts, but we're not there yet!) We can go to meetings twice a day for life, but unless we *use* the program of A.A. to change, we will, at most, be just **undrunk. At** worst, we might remove ourselves from A.A. *unchanged* and either drink or remain the same poor wretch that initially crawled through the doors of Alcoholics Anonymous.

So, if attending meetings is the *only* medicine we take, meeting makers won't make it!

Let's apply this to our relationships. Unless there is *approximate conformity* to A.A.'s Twelve Steps and Twelve Traditions, the individual or the "group" of two or more can *also* wither and die. A friend says: "Just as your *body* can die for lack of nourishment, so can your *relationships*."

"Complacency."

The dictionary defines "complacency" as " a feeling of quiet pleasure or security, often while being unaware of some potential danger," "self-satisfaction," or "smug." It also means "Satisfaction with an existing situation." That is one *powerful* definition of what happens in the relapse process.

This was one *sticky* conversation Bill and I had to have *with both sponsors present*. We were both *recovering alcoholics*, and *alcoholic relapse* was always a possibility. We had to have a mutually agreed-upon plan in place in case one of us relapsed into drinking. We agreed that the person who relapsed and drank would make other living arrangements and leave our home. We each agreed **not** to enable the other to *continue* drinking but to support any recovery efforts made by the drinking alcoholic. This was a document we both signed, and our sponsors were witnesses. Thank God those plans never had to be activated!

My friend Janet and I once co-chaired a weekend Workshop on the 6th and 7th steps called *"Drop the Rock – no, it's my rock!"* The only *attendance* requirement was 20 years of sobriety or more. We were asked to do this Workshop because so many people with a lot of time in recovery became complacent and slowly left the Alcoholics Anonymous program, the program that gave them a second chance at life. "OK, God, I'll take it from here!"

The A.A. Grapevine once printed what it called the **"Reverse Promises"** of the Ninth Step Promises:

"If we are NOT painstaking about this phase of our development, we will be drunk before we leave the parking lot.

We are going to know a new pain and a new misery. We will regret our deeds yet repeat them over and over.

We will comprehend the word chaos, and we will know calamity.

No matter how far down the road we stagger, we will still wonder where we are going. That feeling of uselessness and self-pity will intensify.

We will lose interesting things and gain relations with strange fellows. Self-seeking will be constant. Our whole attitude will be on the lookout for the cops. Fear of people and economic insecurity will leave us homeless. We will intuitively know how to stay drunk with little or no money. We will suddenly begin to think that God does not exist.

Are these extravagant promises? Probably not.

They are being practiced daily, sometimes insanely, sometimes deadly. They will continue to happen if we keep drinking."

That reminds me of the one-car theory. If we were each given only one car for our entire life, no replacement no matter what, we would take *such* good care of that car. We would change the oil regularly, rotate the tires, check the fluids, and continuously wash and polish the vehicle. It would enthusiastically last us for our entire life.

What about *our* one body? What about *our* sobriety? What about *our* one special relationship (or 20 or more, counting friends, children, and co-workers)? ***What about*** *them*? Complacency and neglect don't work to enhance any of these either.

I told you that we established guidelines in case one of us relapsed. Let's talk about the relapse *process*. Of course, drinking alcohol is the last step in the relapse process. *Relapse is a process* taking place over an undetermined period of time. By the time an A.A. member who has been sober a while actually picks up a *drink*, a process of *spiritual disintegration* will have occurred in which the person gradually and subtly withdraws from the spiritual program of Alcoholics Anonymous. For a time, he may still attend meetings and continue to sponsor, but self-centeredness reasserts itself. *Emotionally*, he withdraws more and more. He criticizes and discounts the meetings and the people in the meetings. He spiritually isolates himself. *He is there to get, not give*. He forgets that happiness lies in the giving. He sees only personalities, not principles.

Nothing flows *through* him.

Self-reliance and self-obsession are once again running his show. Intellectually, *he believes his denial*. The *kiss of death* is when I hear, "I know I've cut back on A.A., *but I never think about drinking*." As if the thought of drinking is a warning sign that he could use to avert tragedy. Drinking is the final *solution* to the real problem: the **pain of his obsession with himself!**

If he's a real alcoholic, we all know how well *that* works out!

I once read a book where the hero *"jumped on his horse and rode madly off in all directions."* I've never forgotten that wonderful description of *chaos*. Chaos on the *inside* as well as the *outside*. It's a perfect description of an alcoholic on the downward slide!

The heartbreaking truth is this: the person who relapses is in such denial of reality that by the time a drink appears in his hand, the *decision* to drink is entirely logical. It results from a series of crazy thoughts that started some time ago, perhaps as a resentment left unresolved, a shady behavior he kept to himself, or something else he kept a secret. *Self*, manifested in various negative ways, has set the ball rolling.

We have a daily reprieve. We have a daily reprieve.

It may be clear to everyone around him that he is in serious trouble, but to the *relapsing* alcoholic, his thinking, feelings, and behavior are fine; thank you very much. He accuses everyone else of interfering with his "program of recovery."

Once he has proved that *"those people"* don't understand him and are enemies of his well-being, he can legitimately and self-righteously withdraw from A.A.

The *bedevilments* of self-centeredness overtake him, and ultimately, a drink of alcohol seems the only solution to soothe the pain of his existence. "*I'll show you; I'll hurt me.*" "Cunning, baffling, and powerful." "Alcohol is a subtle foe."

We can only pray that alcohol takes him down quickly and sufficiently so that he gets back into A.A. and sobriety. I have a friend who relapsed after twenty-seven years of sobriety and has been back for three years. She says it is a daily struggle because "*the magic is gone.*" I have to be willing to change in order to *continue* to experience the magic.

So, back to Bill and me and our journey toward emotional sobriety – towards being grown-ups. We started with a knee-to-knee discussion about who should take out the trash! It's amazing how *heated* such a discussion can become! Feelings get hurt, accusations get fired from both sides, walls go up, we stalk away from each other in a huff, and nothing gets resolved.

We will try again another time when one or both sponsors are present, a factor that significantly lessens the volatility of the discussion.

Our growth is accomplished as individuals rather than as a group. Once again, we cannot work on each other's spiritual growth: we can only tend to ourselves and at our own speed.

I need to know myself, my assets and liabilities, how much I'm willing to compromise for the good of the group, and how flexible I can be in any situation. This requires a lot of attention to the *principles* embedded in the Twelve Steps and Twelve Traditions. It requires a lot of one-on-one time with my sponsor. It requires the spotlight to be on *me* and *my* thoughts, feelings, and behaviors. **Love and tolerance of others** is our Code. The spirit of love and service animates them, and a true fellowship is possible, one day at a time.

But before *that* could happen, I had to become aware of some of my childish reactions to life. Much to my chagrin, early in our marriage, I found out I'm a "*thrower*." I threw things when frustrated, hurt, threatened, or interfered with – not at people, windows, or such, but at "safe" places like a door or a blank wall. *I was a thoughtful thrower.*

After trying different items, I refined the art to only throwing wrapped bars of bath soap. I didn't damage anything with the soap; it made no mess, and it could still be used later, dents and all. I called it *smart throwing*!

The last time I threw anything, many years ago, it was as a result of **my reaction** to something Bill said. I just happened to be putting the soap away in a cabinet when he said it. I threw the soap at the door and had a sudden insight: "*You said that just to see what my reaction would be, didn't you?*" He admitted he had baited me and apologized. We both started to laugh. I never threw anything again, and I want to think he never baited me again, either!

As we were "maturing," I stopped being a "thrower," and Bill stopped calling himself a "ducker."

We found that *honest communication* was essential to understanding the guidelines we forged to form a true partnership of equals. I firmly believe that neither of us relapsed into drinking because we *never* stopped working with newcomers and never stopped accepting service commitments. We continued to be active in A.A. events, even when we each *momentarily* crawled back into that tiny ball of self-centeredness, that selfishness that brings about criticism, judgment, and complacency.

Okay – *now*, back to "Who takes out the trash?"

In a healthy, grown-up relationship, all its members must agree on guidelines for acceptable conduct. Both partners must be willing to operate in the relationship with a goal of *unity and growth*, not only for the partnership itself but for the *individuals* who make up that partnership.

Suppose one person begins to behave in an un-acceptable manner or one that is contrary to the agreed-upon guidelines. This may indicate that he no longer values the relationship and sees no reason to make it work. I'm thinking now of someone having an affair, getting obsessed with online pornography, becoming a workaholic, or not being "present" except in body. In these situations, neither party finds the relationship *spiritually beneficial.* This would also hold in the workplace or a friendship, especially the *emotional distancing* of one person from the relationship.

Here's an example of emotional distancing: we hadn't been married very long when we concluded that Bill was in a no-win situation at his job and that he should start his own business. He was very good at it, worked hard, and was very successful. Initially, he had to travel to establish clients for his business and was gone from home for *weeks* at a time. Without realizing it, we reverted to our way of thinking before knowing each other. I don't mean we dated or did anything that wasn't "marriage-approved." I mean, our **thinking** became singular, and our attitude became one of "boss" for each of us. When Bill *was* home, all kinds of maneuvering for control kept us in chaos. This occurred when he was *not* at home, as well. We had both emotionally separated, although we didn't know it intellectually.

When Bill was out of town, he called me every night.

(Remember, we had no cell phones or caller IDs in those days.) Bill called me from wherever he stayed, and I rarely asked the hotel's name. As usual, we argued on the phone one night, and he hung up on me! I felt such *frustration and anger* when I couldn't get back in touch with him to continue the "*discussion* " (to prove I was right, of course. I always had to have the last word). Later, he told me he felt the same irritation, but his ego stopped him from calling me back. *He knew he had control of the situation.* He knew it, and I knew it. Hence, my frustration!

The definition of "frustration" is so telling: "a feeling of dissatisfaction, often accompanied by anxiety or depression, resulting from *unfulfilled needs* or *unresolved problems*." I had spent most of my life in this state of unrest!

It seems I had a filter over my thinking, which ensured I got what I wanted when I wanted it according to my specifications. This filter skews my thinking, so I'm always right, you are always wrong, and I'm in control!

It could have gone either way for us. Fortunately for our little group of two, we both wanted the relationship to work and were amenable to altering our thinking and behavior to accommodate this objective. **Our sponsors were indispensable;** they were the voice of reason while we rode madly off in all directions! *Back* to the exercise of sitting knee to knee, holding hands, inviting God in, saying the Serenity Prayer out loud, and talking in "I" language. It worked every time!

We learned the value of *pausing* when agitated or doubtful. When we were upset, we began to ask ourselves, "How *important is it* in the big picture?" We started to change our perspective about control and needing to be right.

We agreed to stop having arguments over the phone. That took a lot of "restraint of tongue!" We also began to have fewer disagreements at home as we began to apply these same *principles* when we were together.

It was amazing that neither of us was aware of our healthy shift in thinking and feeling; it just happened as we concentrated on practicing the principles of A.A. in our daily lives.

My friend Kathy says, "*When I'm okay with me, I don't have to make you wrong.*"

Sometimes, we just had to laugh at our individual and collective **childishness**! We realized we were not together for power, money, prestige, or security. We were together because we loved each other and for our *individual spiritual growth*.

Voluntarily.

Growth cannot be accomplished as a group; it can only be achieved individually by each person in the group **and** at *their* own pace. In our relationship, no one was the boss or gave orders. We began truly to use spiritual principles to handle our different responsibilities. The Twelve Steps and Twelve Traditions translate beautifully into household chores and principles for living the big picture!

I did the laundry; he took out the trash!

Questions from Tradition Nine

1. *List some of the ways I practice the principles of "love and service" in all my affairs in my daily life.*

2. *Am I able and willing to align my "weltanschauung" (my worldview) with my partner to arrive at mutually agreed-upon solutions to common problems? List two recent examples.*

3. *How am I flexible in my expectations of the other in our relationship? How do I compromise?*

4. *Have I completed a proper 4ᵗʰ step? Have I become truly aware of the nature of my wrongs?*

5. *How do I look at my life and its people, places, and things from an entirely different angle?*

6. *What is that different angle?*

7. *How do I keep an open mind and an open heart in listening to my partner, sponsor, grown child, boss, co-worker, or friend?*

8. *How do I honor what is acceptable and what is not acceptable in my relationships?*

9. *Do I allow unacceptable behavior by having a "peace at any price" attitude? If "Yes," explain.*

10. *How do I practice "love and tolerance of others" in my relationships? How about "live and let live"?*

11. *Explain how we are ultimately together for individual spiritual growth in any meaningful relationship.*

12. *When discussing my ideas about life, do I ask myself, "Who taught me this attitude?" "Is it true for me today?" "Is this an idea that, as a grown-up, I want to keep?"*

13. *How do I practice the slogan, "How important is it?" when I'm upset?*

14. *How do I practice Rule 62? ("Don't take yourself so seriously" in the Twelve x Twelve, Tradition Four.)*

15. *How do I practice genuine acceptance where appropriate, whether I approve or not?*

16. *Do I believe that "meeting makers" need more than meetings? Why? What?*

17. *Have I become complacent about my sobriety, my relationships, and my life? What does "complacent" mean to me?*

18. *If I relapse into drinking, do I have an agreed-upon action plan with my partner, sponsor, boss, friend, or grown child?*

19. *Do I understand the reality of "relapse" as a process, not an event? Explain "relapse." Explain the "process."*

20. *What primary actions can I take to guarantee happy, long-term sobriety?*

Avoid Heated Discussion!

IN THE 12 x 12, the Tenth Tradition states, "Alcoholics Anonymous has no opinion on outside issues; hence, the A.A. name ought never be drawn into public controversy."

For *our* purposes of incorporating the *spirit* of the Traditions into our everyday relationships, the Tenth Tradition could read: "A relationship should avoid heated controversy about outside issues, whether it's as a couple, as friends, with grown children, or the Uber driver on the way to the airport." The *unity* of the relationship can be disrupted and, in some cases, destroyed. We are each entitled to our own opinion on outside issues. The "heated controversy" doesn't have to be about significant outside issues, like how to run a country or manage a football team. It could be about how to fold the laundry, train the dog, or the right way to drive a car.

The essence of this Tradition in relationships is learning to *disagree without being disagreeable*. I remember the first time my sponsor said that. I thought, "That can't be right!" My experience with disagreements had been fighting vigorously and loudly, never giving up or giving in. I did not care that the results were disastrous—**I was right!**

Sobriety is a growth process. I've heard that recovery is like walking up a down escalator: I'm sliding backward unless I'm moving *forward.*

Relationships are like that, too. Controversy is usually a by-product of fear. Almost everything negative is a by-product of self-centered fear!

Life is all about priorities. All my life, *my* **focus** had been to get *what* I wanted *when* I wanted it, regardless of the cost, physically, mentally, or spiritually. I ran like a tornado through not only *my* life but others' lives as well. And when I stepped on the toes of others, and they retaliated, I turned tail and ran. I literally would pack up and move if something or someone upset me.

That happened to me in 1972 in Dallas, Texas, after I went to my first and only A.A. meeting. I didn't go because I thought it was a good idea or because I thought I was an alcoholic. I went because my doctor suggested it. I was so drunk I could hardly drive, and I don't remember anything about the meeting, but it upset me so much that I decided *Dallas* was my problem. I packed my car that night and moved to Florida. It is obvious to me *now* that my **only concern** was to be able to continue drinking, and I changed *everything to* accommodate this priority.

It took me *three long years* before **alcohol** changed my priority, and I **experienced** my powerlessness over alcohol. When I surrendered to my powerlessness and embarked on our program of recovery, my priorities changed. I suddenly wanted to be sober more than I wanted to drink. Even though my only experience with "*sobriety*" during those three years had been miserable, and I had no idea what "sober" meant, I came into A.A. hoping it would be better than what I had! This was not a thoughtful, intellectual decision; it was visceral, a seismic upheaval inside of me where I took a total leap of faith, *which I did not have,* into something *I knew nothing about* and *did not believe would work.*

As a newcomer, I remember reading the Big Book and whining to my sponsor: "I just don't see how this thing works." I had been to psychiatrists, doctors, and counselors over the years to find out why I was so unhappy. From them, I learned how to blame others for my drinking. *I was such a victim!* I came into Alcoholics Anonymous thinking that *if* I could *"get a handle"* on A.A., I could **control** my recovery and get *what* I wanted *when I* wanted it. My sponsor pointed to the title of the 5th chapter entitled, *"**How It Works**."* "Read this," she said. "This is how it works." My whining was over, at least about *that* issue!

In the beginning, it appeared I was living my life in sobriety. But what was happening *inside of me* was a realigning of priorities and values. It became *more* important for me to be at peace than to fight for my right to be right or to pack up and move when I was threatened or hurt. **The *thoughts* and *feelings* were still there, but my *actions* changed.**

To avoid "heated controversy," I must first acknowledge that people are – *real.* I had always treated others as cardboard cutouts on **my** stage. You have heard me talk about the Twelve-Step calls my sponsor dragged me on when I was three weeks sober. I somehow found myself *wanting* to be helpful to these women without needing anything in return. I felt such *joy* when we left their houses. I knew I had been useful – I had passed on as much information about getting sober as I knew. What they did with that information was not my business. *What a concept!* It was so foreign to my way of thinking. My old way was, "They should get sober

and loudly thank me, me, me!" But I **did not** feel that way –
I was beginning to feel happy and usefully whole.

I didn't realize till much later that the joy came from
getting outside myself enough to feel compassion for another
suffering human being. If self-centeredness is the root of
my troubles, the highest form of spirituality is its opposite:
compassion.

My sponsor insisted I join her at the women's meeting,
and it was there that I continued my transformation. The
women's meeting became an important, *safe schoolroom*
to "practice" life, learn how to get outside myself, form a
true friendship, and learn how to give rather than get. I
developed healthy self-respect as I allowed others to see the
real me. I started to lower the mask I had worn all my life to
hide **my belief** that I was a totally inadequate loser and that
if you knew the **real** me, you would abandon me. I slowly
began to set aside this mask when interacting with these
women, individually and as a group.

The mask was called "arrogance," and under the mask
was a frightened and lonely little girl. *As I began to see this
truth about* **me**, *I began to see it about* **you**, *too.*

Upon reflection, I saw I had never made a 100%
commitment to *any* relationship I had ever had. It was always a 99% commitment at best. Do you know what a 99%
commitment is? It's dancing with the love of your life,

looking over his shoulder to see if someone better is coming along! It was exclusively about me, me, me. This included three marriages and countless casual acquaintances.

So, I live on at least **two levels:** the conscious level, using my five senses of seeing, touching, tasting, feeling, or hearing. That is the physical world. That is where I see, observe, judge, and react, either positively or negatively, based on my *judgment.* As a newcomer in A.A., this conscious level was somewhat mechanical, usually negative and fear-based, and almost always coming from the thoughts, feelings, and concepts I learned growing up.

I also have *higher* senses: intuition, perception, imagination, will, memory, and reason. These have nothing to do with my *physical* world.

When I came to A.A., I had no idea how powerful these senses could be, especially when coupled with help from the God of my *experience.* I learned through that experience that I want to open this connection between God and me as widely as possible. When that happens, what flows through that connection is an incredible, powerful, intuitive stream of information from that creative source. I can get answers to questions that used to baffle me. I have a sense of freedom being around other people because it has become more than the shallow, superficial connection I had always had. I can have profound and meaningful loving concerns for people I was incapable of having before A.A.

This is the *second level* on which I live. I didn't realize that most of my learning would be at that ***unconscious*** level.

I use these six attributes (intuition, perception, imagination, will, memory, and reason) at the unconscious level. However, if I become aware of and cultivate and *improve* these skills, with God's help, through the Steps and Traditions of Alcoholics Anonymous, a whole new world opens up to me. I will have entered the world of the spirit. I will have been rocketed into the fourth dimension. I can get outside my puny little self-obsessed self and treat others as I would have them treat me!

However, there's a drawback: I can't just enter the world of the spirit and stay there. I have to renew my membership in the "God-centered" Club every day – I truly have a daily reprieve. It says in the Big Book *that **we can't rest on our laurels***. I looked it up: "To rest on one's laurels" means "to be content with one's past or present achievements." In other words, to become ***complacent.*** In **Tradition Nine**, I wrote about complacency and how insidious, dangerous, and potentially fatal it can be.

Okay, back to the second level of living I was *un-knowingly* experiencing as a newly sober woman. I was following directions I didn't understand, didn't believe, and didn't think would work for me.

But I did it anyway because I wanted to stay sober. I knew *you* knew how to stay sober, and I didn't. And if this was the *crazy way you* did it, I'd do it, too.

At five years sober, I married Bill, who was nine years sober. We scurried back into our little caves of hostile self-centeredness, and chaos reigned! We suddenly had an *adversarial relationship,* and defensive walls were erected with alarming speed! We discovered we had differences in temperament, differences in traditions and training, and different life experiences. *No wonder we were at odds.* We had to recognize that being different is normal. Differences ensure *variety.* However, differences can also produce *conflict.* The conflict can be manageable if there is a 100% commitment to the relationship.

Fortunately, we both had the *only* requirement for **relationship membership**: the desire to be *in* that relationship and the willingness to take the actions necessary to preserve the *unity* of that relationship. Harmony in our home became more important to me than the need to convince Bill that I was right (no matter what) and he was wrong (no matter what).

We began to learn that we each had our own way of thinking and to *accept* those differences. Most of the time, although we differed significantly, each of us was right. We were *both* right. We began to ask ourselves what we were willing to give up to create the partnership we wanted. Our sponsors gave us a list of questions to ask ourselves to keep tabs on our priorities. Here are some of them:

- Do you each work the 12 Steps and 12 Traditions in your marriage?

- Which Steps do you practice in your relationships?

- Which Traditions do you practice at home and outside the home, with friends, grown children, co-workers, bosses, the cashier at the grocery store, and the stranger driving the car in front of you?

- How does *powerlessness* apply in your relationship?

- Have you turned your life, will, partner, and other people over to the care of God?

- Are you as aware of *your* character defects as you are of your partner's?

- Do you take an inventory every day, and **when** you're wrong, promptly admit it?

- Do you treat your spouse, friends, co-workers, and grown children with the same love and tolerance you would treat any *newcomer* in A.A.?

With questions like these, you can see why I had to change my focus to maintaining and growing our marital relationship. I learned to concentrate on *myself and my actions*, not *him*. Once again, I didn't have to wait for *him* to change so *I'd* feel better! I stopped criticizing him to others (except when I was talking to my sponsor, and she always turned the spotlight back on me). Once, after complaining about something Bill had done, she asked me, "I wonder what *you* do that annoys *him*?" Ouch!

I learned there was always a pay-off when I judged harshly or found fault and blamed someone else for my unhappiness. My *motive* – and the *payoff* – is to get sympathy, feel superior, or avoid looking at *my* issues. This attitude further separates me from you; I *already* feel isolated and alone. This attitude stems from what our Big Book calls "*old ideas*." These ideas were formed in childhood, some genetic, some from my environment. They are based on my **perceptions** and the **beliefs** which these perceptions engender.

My habit of blaming others for how I feel is just a resentment in which I don't take responsibility for my life.

This leads to my needing to control other people to make sure I feel all right.

Now, here's a mouthful – it makes perfect sense to me; I hope it makes sense to you. My need for *control* arises from my *opinions*. My *opinions* originate as a result of my *judgments*. My judgments come out of my *thinking. (I told you my problems center in my mind, not my body!). To* find *serenity*, I have to decide to change the *thinking that creates the judgments that lead to my opinions, bringing* about my incessant and impossible need to *control.*

Some form of self-centered fear usually brings about the demand for control. It doesn't matter if the demand is in the marital home, the office, or the grocery store; the results are the same: both sides tend to take an immovable stand to defend their ideas and opinions. Soon, the *defensive stance itself becomes an important issue,* and the ideas and opinions become secondary. There will be *no* backing down, *no* mutual decision to "disagree without being disagreeable." The change in my thinking does not mean I am a people pleaser, a wimp, or a doormat. It means I don't have to engage in every war to which I'm invited, and I don't have to take everything *personally*. It's about knowing that the other person's disagreements are about the other person, not me! Even if they are shouting at *me*, it's still about *them.* Knowing what is mine and what is not mine is about self-respect and respect for others, no matter how loud they are when expressing their disagreement!

Live and let live.

I have been in business meetings of my home group, district meetings, and area assemblies where many attendees were hostile and unpleasant. All were vying for control of *something!* I've written about this in earlier chapters. Especially in a romantic relationship, debate and disillusionment can arise because of misplaced or largely uncommunicated expectations.

Bill and I discovered, through professional counseling, that our significant sources of conflict revolved around a few major issues: sexual issues, money issues, helping around the house issues, mutual respect issues, and preoccupation with job issues.

Suppose we add our differences in temperament, the training and traditions we each received growing up, and differences in life experiences. No wonder two people who love each other can have such difficulties. We found that relationship adjustments are not automatic just because we want them; they are a *learned skill, an art form.* Who knew? The first requirement is that we each had to quit playing God. Above all, we must learn to communicate about our issues *when they arise*, not three months later!

So many times, there is no right or wrong; there are just differences of opinions. I've learned I must allow the other person the right to have these differences and *the right to be wrong*. I learned that we could have differences of opinion about the *same situation* and that we can both be comfortable with these dissimilarities. I have learned to concentrate not on our differences but on our humanity, common bonds, and places where we agree. In the past, I could only see the differences, not the *person* behind the differences. I would heatedly argue my side as if I were defending my life!

Upon reflection, and with the help of my sponsor, I traced this attitude and subsequent behavior back to my relationship with my parents, particularly with my alcoholic father. He was as volatile as I was. He and I would take on heated arguments about anything as if it were a badge of honor. There was no sense of humor or healthy perspective about what we were doing. We would stomp angrily away from each other and not speak for long periods of time. This was especially true if the argument was about political matters *over which we had no control,* but actually, any subject would do.

The demand to be right is such a significant characteristic of the alcoholic.

Unity is still my goal in any relationship. "We have ceased fighting anyone or anyone. We have entered the world of the spirit." This is not to say I can make every relationship harmonious, and I am *not a doormat*. It takes two to tango. When I run into someone with no interest in harmony, I smile, wish them well, and go on with my life. I don't take it personally because it's not about *me*. It is definitely about them. What's mine and what's not – how freeing is that? How free do I want to be?

So I can practice these principles in all my affairs. Notice that I say, "I can," I don't say I always do. *Practice* and *repetition* are still two of my favorite spiritual tools.

With repetition, we discover things for ourselves. Here's an example: I've been sponsoring a woman for a long time. One day, she ran up to me before a meeting and said, "Guess what I learned at the meeting last night?" She then described the principle I'd been talking to her about for months! Hearing about it from me repeatedly, and probably from others in the program, she heard it when she was ready. She discovered it for herself. I tell her that is wonderful, and we go into the meeting together.

I wonder how many times I've done that to my sponsor and how many more times *I* will have that same kind of discovery through repetition.

Now, I want to talk about a variation on controversy and my need to be right no matter the cost. My inclination in a war is to gather up my troops and attack the enemy. I'm talking about any situation where I feel vulnerable and my false pride is on the line. I must win at any cost. So here's my variation: in any personal, intimate relationship, marriage, or perfect friendship, whining about our problems on the sly to people outside the relationship is **_major_** passive-aggressive behavior. This results in a situation where those not involved are taking sides and casting votes at a public level. This can only increase the existing friction and further erode unity!

This is scorekeeping at its worst! Before sobriety and well into sobriety, my habit had always been to tell everyone about the *injustices* heaped upon me by my parents, boyfriend, husband, teacher, friend, policeman, clerk in a store, and the family dog. I solicited sympathy and votes in my favor. I wanted *everyone* to know the truth and be on my side.

I saw no reason *not* to continue this practice after Bill and I married. It always made me feel warm and fuzzy when I would pour out my heart to someone about some misdeed Bill had done and hear, "Oh, you poor long-suffering dear. Let me give you a hug."

One vote for me!

My sponsor stopped me cold one day when I began to solicit *her* vote on some offense Bill had committed. "This is dishonest and unloving behavior," she said. "If you two are a *united* group of two, you must do nothing that will destroy that unity. ***Gossip*** is a sure way to do that." "I'm not gossiping; I'm sharing the truth with you," I said righteously. She replied, "Gossip is character assassination, and you are spreading only *your* opinion of the situation to others. I know you are so insecure that you must drag him down to feel okay about yourself. Still, in the bigger picture, you are killing any possibility of creating a loving and harmonious relationship with Bill or anybody else when you use these manipulative tactics."

I reluctantly realized she was right. I had not looked at it that way. *She took all the fun out of it* as she always did when presenting me with a truth I had to acknowledge even when I didn't want to! After these sessions, I would always feel sorry for myself and resent the object of my discomfort, *Bill*. Isn't that strange? I should have been uncomfortable with *myself* because I was in the wrong, but it was such a comfortable old habit to point the finger and blame others. Then I would emerge from my self-imposed and self-centered funk and ask myself, "What can I do about it **today**?" My answer was always to get on my knees and ask God for help with the **now** uncomfortable issue of gossiping. ***God's answer*** was always the same: to focus my attention on someone *outside of me*, like a woman I sponsor or a woman at a meeting who was new to A.A. and ***really*** uncomfortable. "How can I be helpful?" became my slogan for the day.

When I am given new insight into myself, I have to examine my behaviors and their motivation. This is almost always accompanied by *ego deflation* and another *surrender*.

There is a prayer by Thomas Merton, which is one of my favorites. It is a prayer for surrender.

"My lord God, I have no idea where I'm going. I do not see the road ahead of me. I cannot know for certain where it will end. Nor do I really know myself, and the fact that I *think* I am following your Will does not mean that I am actually doing so. But I do believe that the desire to please you does, in fact, please you. And I hope that I have that desire in all that I am doing. I hope that I will never do anything apart from that desire. And I know if I do this, you will lead me by the right road, though I may know nothing about it. So I will trust you always, though I may seem to be lost and in the shadow of death. I will not fear, for you are ever with me, and you will never leave me to face my perils alone."

Surrendering to the daily practice of our Twelve Steps puts our lives in order, but not necessarily our relationships. How to live successfully with others can be found in our Traditions.

The unique Traditions of Alcoholics Anonymous were born out of the desire to preserve our fellowship for future generations of sick and suffering alcoholics. The founders were drunks who shared their experiences with each other about getting sober and staying sober. Initially, there were no guidelines or directions on how to accomplish this goal. The first directions, the Twelve Steps, were evolved from their own experiences. Our founders continued to stumble along, making mistakes but *staying sober*, coming up with terrible ideas about the influence they could have all over the world, and *staying sober*. The Traditions are the ground-breaking conclusions they drew when examining their many mistakes and *staying sober*.

The Traditions I practice in my personal life come from the same sources: my new and ground-breaking experiences coupled with the desire to stay sober and to learn how to be of maximum service to God and those around me.

Just as it was with our founders, sometimes I have to think about or do something wrong before *learning* how to do it right. These are my *old ideas* surfacing in situations where they are not needed or appropriate. They are now, and always have been, *counter-productive!* Over the years, I have learned to talk to someone, usually my sponsor, **before** taking action on these old ideas.

The Traditions that the early A.A.'s created out of trial, error, and necessity are my signposts and my guidance along the route.

Tradition Ten delves deeply into the concept of "*Live and Let Live*," a slogan that is essential to the well-being of *any* relationship. Just like our founders, *I can't do it alone.* I need to *learn* how to be in harmonious relationships with my God, the people of Alcoholics Anonymous, and everyone on the planet as I trudge my road of happy destiny.

Chapter Ten

Questions from Tradition Ten

1. *How do I practice the slogan "Live and Let Live" in every relationship, no matter how temporary?*

2. *What does this slogan mean to me?*

3. *How do I work on my own recovery program rather than my partner's?*

4. *Do I practice Tradition Ten in all my affairs? Why? How?*

5. *How does powerlessness apply in my relationships?*

6. *Have I turned my life, my will, my **partner, and everyone else** over to the care of God?*

7. *Am I as aware of my character defects as I am of my partner's? Give some examples.*

8. *Do I take an inventory every day, and when I'm wrong, promptly admit it? How do I do this inventory?*

9. *Do I still blame others for how I feel? Why?*

10. *How do I treat every relationship, especially the one with my partner, with the same love and tolerance that I treat any newcomer in A.A.?*

11. *What do I get if I continue to be a victim?*

12. *Without feeling rejected or becoming defensive, do I allow my partner to disagree with my ideas?*

13. *Do I often have heated arguments with my partner? Is there a recurring issue that initiates the controversy? Why is it recurring and not resolved?*

14. Do I pause when agitated or doubtful to avoid an unnecessary argument, or do I immediately begin to defend myself?

15. Is it important for me to always be right? Why?

16. Can I "disagree without being disagreeable?" What does this mean to me?

17. Do I gossip negatively about my partner to anyone who will listen? Do I collect "sympathy votes? Am I still a victim?

18. Have I made amends for the harm I have caused by my past struggles for control in my relationships?

19. What A.A. tools can I use to avoid an argument before it begins?

20. How do I practice "Live and Let Live" in every relationship, no matter how temporary?

Judged by Our Actions!

TRADITION ELEVEN IN the 12x12 states: "Our public relations policy is based on attraction rather than promotion;
we need always maintain personal anonymity at the level of
press, radio, and films."

Regarding living the Traditions in relationships,
Tradition Eleven could be stated this way: "We communicate our belief system through our actions rather than
what we say. Our behavior should be based on attraction
rather than promotion." An element of humility runs

through *all* our Traditions, but it is especially strong in Tradition Eleven.

I can ask myself if *my* behavior is attractive, not only to others but to **me**. I remember complaining to my sponsor one day about something Bill had done, and she had the nerve to ask me, "I wonder what *you* do that annoys *him*?"

I didn't want to even *think* about this possibility. What would I see if I looked at myself through Bill's eyes? Would I find my behavior and attitude attractive? Would I find my words full of love and tolerance, or would they be full of judgment and criticism? Would I find that I'm a generous person—generous with my time, my attention, and my affection? Do I radiate harmony or chaos?

After this painful conversation with my sponsor, I started taking an inventory by asking myself those questions to see how attractive *I* was. If the answers were all negative, thank goodness I already had the solutions built into the questions!

The Eleventh Tradition talks about anonymity. At the core of the disease of alcoholism is obsessive self-absorption and extreme self-centeredness. The opposite is humility, selflessness, and anonymity. The Traditions are a roadmap of how to get from self-absorption to humility, from lonely and isolated fear to connectedness. Anonymity in a relationship is:

"The ability to do good for good's sake and not have to take credit for it." It is a long and winding road.

When I came to A.A., I lived inside my isolated self. I totally identified with my thoughts, feelings, and compulsive patterns of perception. This was the base from which I viewed the world, and everything in that world was about me, me, me.

Here are some concrete examples: If a friend died, I told everybody how *I* was affected and how *I* felt, with no awareness of how this sad event touched others. If it rained and I wanted to go to the beach, I would be full of self-pity. "Why does this always happen to me?" I cried. If the stoplight turned red and I was in a hurry, I felt resentment and despair (same self-centered reasoning as with the rain event). If you left me, I would be a victim and overwhelmed with resentment. I whined about how cruel you were to me, never thinking about what I did to facilitate your leaving. If I thought you slighted me, I was deeply hurt emotionally and didn't consider the possibility that your dog had just died, and you were preoccupied and didn't even see me. If *you* achieved recognition in the home, the office, or anywhere else, I wallowed in resentment and self-pity ("It should have been me, me, me."). If *I* was promoted or acknowledged in some way, I boasted about how deserving and superior I was and how I beat you in this game of life.

I took everything personally. My focus was always on me. When I came to A.A., I didn't see for a long time that this perception gave everything *outside* of me complete control over me, me, me.

I came to believe that the more I tried to control someone or something, the more *I* was controlled. This was because my self-esteem depended on whether you did or didn't do whatever I wanted you to do. As a child, I was taught to place my happiness/unhappiness *outside* of myself. I suffered with an almost unconscious, ever-present anxiety, knowing that I had no real power to control anything but believing that I *should* have that power and that I was a failure if you didn't do as I demanded. In reality, things outside myself had the power, and I had given it away.

Think about it. I gave power to the *rain* to affect how I felt!

Of course, I was completely unaware of any of this. I've heard that a fish doesn't know it's living in water until it's taken out of the water. I had no idea of the enormous bondage of self in which I had been immersed all my life until I began to break free of it in A.A.

To be truly conscious, I must step back from my compulsive identification with my isolated self. Wisdom is an acceptance of the full reality of what *is* right here, right now. The result is a deep joy and a sense of coherent beauty. I have had transitory moments of this wisdom; I know you have, too. For a while, I believed I was *supposed* to be this way *all* the time and thought I was doing recovery wrong when I would fall off that lofty pedestal and show my humanity. My sponsor said if I stayed there all the time, I would take that serenity for granted and wouldn't have the appreciation and gratitude I had when this connectedness happened fleetingly. I was off the perfectionist hook!

When I was newly sober, my sponsor gave me an assignment: "Do something nice for someone every day and don't let them know you've done it." *Do you know how hard that is?* I was living with my father, so I tried to do something nice for him every day. The "don't let him know you've done it" was the hard part. Before this "assignment," I would help by folding the clean laundry, but I would leave it all folded where he could see it and make an appropriate comment about what a good person I was. Then, I would put the laundry away. *I was promoting my worthiness!*

The terms "anonymity" and "attraction rather than promotion" are the same things when I think about it.

Both principles are based on selflessness, humility, and love. This loss of self is the central characteristic of a spiritual life. Letting go is liberation: liberation *from* old ideas and liberation *for* spiritual growth. It is acceptance of the other person in the relationship for who he is at this moment, warts and all. It is me accepting myself for who I am at this moment, warts and all. Throughout my sober life, if I persevere in seeking this spiritual way of life, I will have many instances of **defeat** of self, **surrender** of self, and re-emergence into a new **freedom** from self.

See how the spirit of anonymity floats through this entire discussion about seeking a spiritual way of life? Of course, I didn't call it that. I called it "sobriety." I found it attractive in you and didn't realize I was acquiring a little bit of that essence because I was no longer living isolated inside myself and beginning to feel connected to you.

All my learning is symbolic. I never understand the lesson as it happens. I only see it through *introspective hindsight*, sometimes quickly, sometimes slowly. Years later, I understood the enormous symbolic importance of the women's meeting I attended early in my sobriety. I didn't grasp the colossal significance of my early childhood "lessons" about what was right and wrong in life until I was a member of Alcoholics Anonymous. I noticed I was having difficulty with relationships in A.A. With the Steps and Traditions and lots of help from sponsors and mentors; I began to unravel my past life and look at it from an entirely different angle. I began to see some of the self-defeating patterns I imposed on my life.

I was trapped by what I had experienced in my past and my biased interpretation of those experiences. There is no way to be free of these biases except through spiritual awakenings. I didn't wake up each morning thinking, "I wonder where I'll let go of self-centeredness today?" Or, "I wonder where I'll grow spiritually today?" No, I hesitantly began to try to do the next right thing right, usually at my sponsor's direction. This willingness brought about the shifts in perception so essential to spiritual progress.

Of course, some of these lessons took place *after* I had unilaterally taken some action, suffered the consequences, and *then* told my sponsor about it!

Every event in my life is just a situation in which I am responsible for my response. All my life, I had reacted, not responded. This is the bondage of self at its worst. Reacting is a learned response; it was all I knew when I came to A.A.

When Bill and I were first married, I carefully pointed out every mistake he made. How else was he going to improve? I tried diligently to show him how wrong he was in his opinions and biases.

I told him how improperly he was living his life and how it would be much better and he would be so much happier if he only listened to me and did it my way.

Of course, he gave me the same good advice based on *his* standards!

We both **reacted** to everything, although we didn't call it that. When we would get into one of our many "discuss-ions," we each tried to "promote" our ideas. There was no attraction to it! Communication would break down, and we would end up shouting at each other. We insisted the other person was making us feel and act in a certain way (how's *that* for giving away our power). We would pout and continue to punish the other even when we wanted to make up. We would wait for the other person to apologize first because neither of us would give in – an apology meant defeat in our little marital war.

Our sponsors first pointed out that *someone* had to open the doors of communication, and it took a more spiritually evolved person to do that. You can guess what happened: we fell all over ourselves, throwing wide the doors of reconciliation! We each wanted to be seen as the more "spiritually evolved." How ego-driven was that?

I've written about the assignment our sponsors gave us that changed our lives and enabled us to become "responders" rather than "reactors."

Our assignment was to sit, knee to knee, holding hands. We recited the Serenity Prayer out loud, invited God into our group of two and began expressing ourselves.

Now, however, we had rules!

- We had to empathize with the other person's feelings and thoughts and consider the background from which these thoughts and feelings originated.

- We didn't have to agree with the other's thoughts and feelings; we just had to understand where they came from.

- We had to echo what the other person said: "What I heard you say was this." I was surprised how often what I heard was not what he said.

- I was to stop planning my killer answer while he was talking! No wonder I often heard incorrectly – I wasn't listening!

- I was not to express my feelings and thoughts at this time; it wasn't my turn. I was not to judge what he said, make accusations, or demand that he defend his thoughts and feelings.

- One of our biggest problems was our defensiveness. We felt we had to defend ourselves even when no one made accusations. We learned that defensiveness is often a sign of insecurity, in which *fear* is the controlling factor.

- We could only begin to talk after the other was finished. Along the same lines, we couldn't "Yes, but" each other like a newcomer does when reacting to a suggestion or a comment; "Maybe you could...*Yes, but*" followed by a reason she couldn't possibly follow your suggestion.

- We couldn't bring to the table all the rotten things the other had done in the past; we could only talk about the current issue.

- We couldn't sulk, play the martyr, get angry, or leave. When we do any of these things, we lose sight of what we were talking about initially, and an argument is imminent. We must call a "cease fire" and begin the process again, sitting knee to knee...

We learned that when we let go of negative, knee-jerk reactions and use affirmative communication skills, we could talk rationally and arrive at mutually agreed-upon solutions. As time went on, we learned even more positive ways of communicating.

As a friend of mine says, "I have become *response-able!* Able to respond." I am now thinking beyond the needs of my fearful self. This dramatically improves my self-esteem, which is not even a distant cousin of self-seeking!

The Big Book and the Second Tradition suggest we pause when agitated or doubtful. "Agitated means excited" or "disturbed." Where's God in that? I can get in trouble when I'm excited because my emotions are running high, I'm running the show, and I am sometimes out of control. *"Thy will be done"* is not even on my radar when I'm excited. I'm more alert for this than when I am "disturbed." I'm always aware of being disturbed, and knee-jerk reactions occur – fight or flee. Where's God in that?

Bill and I began to learn how to respond rather than react to each other. Soon, we could each take this new skill to other areas of our lives, such as people we sponsored, our children, our co-workers, friends, and casual encounters. It's amazing how these relationships seemed to improve as well. Who actually changed? I did. Bill did.

Repetition. Restraint of tongue and pen. Repetition. "Thy will be done." Repetition.

Relieved of the need to "win," I find that conflict and controversy get in the way of my primary purpose, to stay sober and carry A.A.'s message of hope to other suffering alcoholics.

I have choices, a million choices a day. My options are either positive or negative. *I am always moving toward or away from a drink of alcohol through my incremental decisions.* Sobriety is like walking up a down escalator: if I'm not moving forward, I am sliding backward.

Through Alcoholics Anonymous, I've come to believe in my connectedness to God, the Universe, and each person in it. A by-product of this new belief is the knowledge that I don't have to make any of these choices using the thinking of the GREAT-I-AM. Solitary self-reliance always fails me. I have sponsors, mentors, friends, my past sober experiences, and sometimes professionals to help me in making my life choices.

I have turned to a therapist, a professional, four times for short-term help during difficult times in my sobriety. In the beginning, this was at my sponsor's suggestion. I was of a mind to arrogantly declare that A.A. had the answer to all my problems. And so it does: on page 133 of our Big Book, it clearly states: "God has abundantly supplied this world with fine doctors, psychologists, and practitioners of various kinds. Do not hesitate to take your health problems to such persons. We should never belittle a good doctor or psychiatrist. Their services are often indispensable."

Each time I availed myself of their services, I was able to clarify "the exact nature of my wrongs" in terms of the thinking, judgment, and opinions that had ruled me all my life.

I know; I've spent many pages writing about Tradition Eleven and haven't even mentioned Tradition Eleven. But I *have* been talking about Tradition Eleven. I've been talking about deflating my ego at depth, of anonymity at its finest.

I've been talking about learning to emphasize *principles*, not individual members (especially me). The whole is greater than the sum of its parts. When just a part of a unified group, each individual becomes an active guardian of that fellowship. This is true whether it's a group of two in a partnership, a friend, an A.A. group, a grown child, a business, or a clerk at the grocery store.

I'm grateful I had five years of unknowingly practicing other-centeredness in my daily sober life before Bill and I began our "group of two" experience!

With the guidance of my sponsor, I began to accept others *as they are* and to accept myself as well. Self-acceptance is essential. I read this somewhere: "Be kind and speak gently to past versions of myself that didn't know the things I know now."

By acting "as if" I already am the person I am trying to become and by putting into practice the principles of Alcoholics Anonymous in my daily life, I am more apt to attract you to my spiritual way of life than if I continuously point out all the ways you are not living up to my spiritual expectations.

All I have to do is look at my sponsor's attitude for confirmation of this principle. She was obviously more spiritually advanced than I was, but she never pointed this out to me and never told me I was doing it wrong because I wasn't at her level of enlightenment. She told me an A.A. fact: *"You can't make a flower grow by pulling on it."*

Preaching doesn't work. It doesn't work with me, and it doesn't work with most people. We raise the drawbridge over the moat, smile sweetly, and pretend the preacher isn't there!!

Walking the walk works so much better than just talking the talk. However, I've found that *both* my angels and demons are good teachers. I know I'm not spiritually fit when I make a wonderfully wise comment in a discussion meeting, and no one says how insightful I am and how my comment changed their life forever. Instead, some newcomer will say the same thing and get rave reviews. This stings more if it's something I've told the newcomer! I conveniently forget that everything I've learned is from someone else.

So I sulk and decide I'll never open my mouth again, and besides, this is not a good meeting after all. This isn't good if I'm talking about my home group!

Thankfully, I don't mention these gripes out loud to the group. I take them to my sponsor or good sober friend, and we laugh about how overly sensitive, ego-driven, and childish I still am. I willingly ask God for help with my negative self-centered thoughts and continue to go to my home group, the best group in the world.

That is a good example of my sober feet in action: *it doesn't matter what I think or feel; it's what I do that counts!*

I have learned that I still act on the old ideas that come from low self-esteem and false pride. Hopefully, I become willing to talk to my sponsor, examine my mistakes, and go to the God of my *experience* to help me correct them.

Through continuing to face these same demons and talking about them, my thinking gradually changes, so those thoughts are no longer driving me. But guess what? My ego-driven pettiness reared its ugly head at my home group *just last week!* I said something brilliant, nobody commented, a newcomer said the same thing, everybody commented, and my feelings were hurt. I had to snitch on myself to my sponsor. She said, lovingly and laughingly, 'Keep coming back, Rena; God isn't finished with you yet."

Wisdom is just another way of seeing and knowing, letting go of my cherished notions about "How things ought to be."

To reveal something new, I have to get rid of the old. *Wanting* a new way will not make it happen. Only moving the old ideas out of the way can do that. *"Insight without action is fantasy."*

I clear out the old – old ideas, old stories I tell myself, old ways of thinking, especially those ideas to which I've become overly attached.

Some of my old ideas include:
- The need to always be right.
- The need to control people, places, and things.
- The need to be self-sufficient.
- The need to judge everybody, including myself.
- The need to be perfect.

I must make room for a new vision in my head, heart, and soul.

Repetition is the surest way of changing these old ideas. As you know, when I was newly sober, my sponsor suggested I do something nice for someone **every day** without letting them know I've done it. This was her subtle way of teaching me to get outside myself. This was hard to do in the beginning, and at that time, I didn't see any value in it, but I persevered.

Paradoxically, she also insisted I find some assets about myself to put on a gratitude list, not just a list of things *outside* of me that I was grateful for. I needed help finding assets. Finally, she suggested that I put at the top of the list that I was sober and grateful for the gift of sobriety.

When Bill and I married and suited up for marital war, she suggested I write a gratitude list about ***Bill*** **every day** and do something nice for **Bill every day** without letting him know. Sometimes, it was through gritted teeth, but I did as my sponsor suggested. I did it because I could look at our history together and remember the experience of her ideas working while mine did not. If nothing changes, nothing changes.

The daily accumulation of these actions helped change my attitude, thoughts, and feelings about Bill and the desirability and efficacy of marital war.

Maybe it's because of the little exercises in anonymity my sponsor had me perform repetitiously; perhaps it's God working on my character defects; maybe it's consciously growing up in the program of Alcoholics Anonymous, but over the years, it has become easier not to have to take credit for the things I've done. Just as *"How important is it?"* works well in avoiding needless arguments, it can also work well in achieving peace and humility. Just as I can bypass taking credit, I can sidestep blame: "Did you see what your husband/child/dog/coworker/friend did?"

Not my circus, not my monkey!

So what does Tradition Eleven have to do with me, me, me?

Everything! Everything!

Questions from Tradition Eleven

1. *Are you convinced to your innermost selves that you are an alcoholic? Why? How?*

2. *Trace the beginning of your alcohol problem*

3. *Can you trace the progression of your alcohol problem?*

4. *Did you ever try to quit drinking on your own? How successful were you? What happened?*

5. *What was **your** miracle, **your** moment of truth?*

6. *How do you feel about A.A. being a spiritual program? Have your feelings changed over time? How have they changed?*

7. *Can you name the qualities your higher power would have to have for you to trust that power? Write a list of seven characteristics – seven words – that describe this higher power. (Not a misprint – a reminder!)*

8. *Do you pray? What is prayer?*

9. *Do you do a daily evening review? (even if you do it in the morning?)*

10. *Do you meditate daily? Even for two minutes? (What is meditation?) Do you listen for intuitive thoughts, direction, and clarity?*

11. *Do you have a plan of action for the day? (This is subject to change without notice, of course. We have to live life on life's terms!)*

12. *Do you write your daily action plan using categories that fit you?*

13. *Do you incorporate "par" into your daily life?*

    Pause: when agitated or doubtful

    Ask: ask for the right thought or action

    Remember: You're no longer running your own show. (This avoids fear, anxiety, anger, worry, self-pity, and foolish decisions.)

It's About the Message!

TRADITION TWELVE IN the Twelve and Twelve states: "Anonymity is the spiritual foundation of all our traditions, ever reminding us to place principles before personalities."

For our purposes, Tradition Twelve could read: "Anonymity is the spiritual foundation of our sober lives, ever reminding us to place principles before personalities."

What is anonymity? What is a foundation? What is a *spiritual* foundation? What is a principle? Which personalities?

Even though I absolutely love the dictionary, I'm one of those people who will read something, know all the words, and assume I know the meaning of the definition.

I can completely miss the point if I'm not careful.

The dictionary defines anonymity this way: "Unknown, usually by choice; unselfishly concerned for the welfare of others." This, of course, is the opposite of self-absorption. If the root of our troubles is self-centeredness, the opposite would be the spirit of anonymity.

Another word for anonymity is *humility*.

As a newcomer, I remember hearing, "I came into A.A. an egomaniac and worked my way up to servant."

To be a sober servant means to me to be willing to do for others what they *cannot* do for themselves and *not* to do for others what they can do for themselves. There is a lot about dignity and grace in that attitude for both parties!

I've written previously about the need to be *self-*centered in a healthy way, a stance where I let the God within me work without me.

I came into A.A. as a victim – a victim of the opinions of other people. I looked up "victim" in my dictionary. You'll never guess what it says: "A person who is deceived or cheated, as by his or her own *emotions,* by the dishonesty of others." It's from the Latin word *victima,* "sacrificial animal."

I was a casualty of my own feelings! The word "cheated" in that definition really hit home. I had unknowingly cheated myself because I deceived myself with negative, self-centered feelings. I placed myself in a position to be hurt. Ouch!

How about this: I looked up "opinion:" "A belief or judgment based on grounds *insufficient* to produce complete certainty; a personal view, attitude, or appraisal."

I lived my life based on faulty beliefs. Those beliefs, these opinions were in **my** head, not yours. They were my interpretation, my opinion, about what I *thought* was your opinion. Of course, I never asked you what your opinion was; I just knew I was right. Crazy but true!

I either acquiesced or revolted, but either way, my perceived opinions of other people ruled my life. That is such a clear example of my *self*-center being *outside* of me. Here is a more truthful way to say that: *I was ruled by my feelings about the opinions I **thought** you had about me.*

I gave control of me to you!

In the Twelfth Tradition, we learn that anonymity is the spiritual foundation of our sober lives, ever reminding us to place principles before personalities. Paradoxically, I was totally self-absorbed, so there was nothing spiritual about my attitude about God, you, and me – it was all about me, me, me, even though I blamed you, you, you!

Through the repetition of *changed behavior*, my God-center was slowly moved back *inside* of me where it had been since before I was born. I finally understood the wisdom of the saying: "What I am looking for, I am looking with!" I began to grasp the concept of what's mine and what's not mine.

Practice, practice, practice!

What is a foundation? What is a *spiritual* foundation? A foundation is the basis of anything. It is the bedrock upon which a structure is built.

"Spiritual" means "of or relating to the spirit or soul, as distinguished from the physical."

My spirit, my soul, has to be the base on which the structure of my sober life rests.

Okay, so far, I find I have to have an unselfish concern for the welfare of others as the bedrock upon which my sober life (and, therefore, every relationship) is built.

What about *principles*? The dictionary says a principle is "a guiding sense of the requirements and obligations of right conduct; a fundamental truth from which others are derived."

It seems the spirit of anonymity is the principle from which we must live our lives, the North Star from which we navigate our behavior in this life of sobriety and internal serenity. Before coming to Alcoholics Anonymous, my guiding principle, my foundational belief system, was fear-based hostility and defensiveness. I had to overcome *you* to get what I wanted, and when I won, it was never enough. I had a "dog eat dog" mentality. I was constantly exhausted from the never-ending battle to protect my "rights" from you, whatever those rights might be.

The principles I've learned and incorporated into my life from the Twelve Steps and Twelve Traditions are simple: they are all about love and tolerance of others. Some call it the Golden Rule (Do unto others as you would have them do unto you). I ask God to help me give to others the same love and tolerance he has given me.

Practicing these principles is accomplished by applying these Twelve Steps and Twelve Traditions as a way of life *every day*. I had to put them *inside* of me for the same reason I used to put alcohol inside of me: *to feel better*.

Now to the big question: what do personalities have to do with the Twelfth Tradition?

Let's go back to the dictionary: *Personality* is "the sum total of the physical, mental, emotional and social characteristics of an individual."

This means that when I am in conflict with another, whether it is a single person or a person as part of a group, the sum total of my physical, mental, emotional, and social characteristics are in a struggle with the sum total of your physical, mental, emotional, and social characteristics.

This is getting complicated.

Is it any wonder there is discord and antagonism between two individuals, and collisions occur when their *sums* are incompatible? Usually, neither party is aware that *this* is the problem underlying the conflict! Usually, each person thinks the *issue* they are fighting about is the problem when it is almost always a *personality difference.*

There are two ways to look at this: your personality or mine. When I am in conflict with another person or group of persons, my personality is encountering another personality that is equally positive that their way is right. Both belief systems are on the line and each party feels threatened unless their personality gains the uppermost hand.

No wonder we are so sensitive and take everything personally! As the Big Book says, "It takes some of us a long time to get over [our sensitivity]." This sensitivity is the immature position of the "undrunk" alcoholic, whether the alcoholic is a member of A.A. or not.

Imagine my surprise when I discovered that the personality I had to place principles before was sometimes *mine!*

I could understand practicing the principle of love and tolerance on some obnoxious idiot in a meeting, smugly saying to myself, "I am practicing the principles of A.A.

over the personality of this fool. I am all good. He is all bad. I am the superior person."

I placed a gold star on my mental report card for *that* day!

But sometimes, *I* was the obnoxious idiot, and I had to dial it back and practice the principles of love and tolerance above *my* personality.

Spiritual growth has its roots in the principle of humility. One definition of humility is "teachability." I began to be able to learn from other people, *whether I liked them or not.* I learned to listen to the message and *not* focus on the messenger. I knew I had to become open and willing to hear God's message regardless of how God chose to send that message to me. I've found that most people are doing the best they can with the knowledge they have at that time, and where they are *spiritually* at that moment.

This includes me. I had to practice love and tolerance of *me,* too!

I came into Alcoholics Anonymous with all the negative personality characteristics I had carefully adopted and groomed since I was a frightened little girl. It took me a long time in A.A. to become *aware* of these character defects, much less to become willing to ask God for help with those characteristics that stood in the way of my usefulness to him.

I always need to remember to include the fact that I have personality *assets* as well as personality *liabilities*. I tend to forget to mention it because my defects get me in trouble, my assets don't. I heard someone say, "My character defects never go away; they just go offstage and change costumes." It was my defects that needed to change. My assets did not need **changing; they** needed **enhancing**.

When I first started talking reasonably honestly with my sponsor, all I could do was tell her how awful I was, how bad I had been, and how little hope there was for me. I was the worst! (I was always an extremist: if I couldn't be the best best, I had to be the best worst!)

When I was a newcomer, my sponsor asked me to make a list of my assets. I couldn't come up with one asset. She said, "Put sober at the top of your list." That broke the ice, and I slowly added that I was kind to animals, I was prompt, and I was trying to eliminate profanity (that was one of the first things I could change on my own, and it made me feel good about myself – I did have some power, after all!)

It was helpful to think of my assets while I was busy beating myself up as the best of the worst! I've discovered that at the core of my being, I really wanted, no, *needed* to be **perfect** in this life, and tended to be unforgiving when I'm not, which is most of the time.

I have found that I must include myself in that "love and tolerance" thing.

In the beginning, I practiced being my real self with "safe" people, like my sponsor or another "old timer." In A.A., I figured they would tolerantly accept me as a newcomer and not take offense when I hesitantly peeked out from behind my well-worn self-protective shield. I knew that no one could ask me to leave A.A. because they didn't like me. I had read the Tradition about the requirements for membership and knew that being likable was not one of them. I had the only requirement for membership – the desire to stop drinking, so I could stay in A.A. no matter what.

This is what Tradition Twelve means to me: I had to find and nurture in my soul (my spiritual foundation) the fundamental truth (the spirit of humility) of being unselfishly concerned for the welfare of others (anonymity). This fundamental truth would guide my behavior in this fledgling life of sobriety. The totality of my physical, mental, emotional, and social characteristics (personality) had to be love and tolerance of others.

So I had to *learn* to be unselfishly concerned about the welfare of others. This was to become *my* fundamental truth, my spiritual foundation from which my behavior would be guided in my sober life. My personality had to change from one of hostility and defensiveness to one of love and tolerance of others.

St. Francis' prayer says it better than I can:

"Lord, make me a channel of thy peace –
that where there is hatred, I may bring love –
that where there is wrong, I may bring the spirit
of forgiveness – that where there is discord,
I may bring harmony – that where there is error,
I may bring truth – that where there is doubt,
I may bring faith – that where there is despair
I may bring hope – that where there are shadows,
I may bring light – that where there is sadness,
I may bring joy.
Lord, grant that I may seek rather to comfort
than to be comforted – to understand rather
than to be understood – to love than to
be loved.
For it is by self-forgetting that one finds. It is by
forgiving that one is forgiven. It is by dying that
one awakens to eternal life.
Amen"

I like to think that by "dying," St. Francis means shedding the "bondage of self." This preoccupation with self blocks me from the sunlight of the spirit, and I am left with only self-reliance to guide me. We all know how well that works! I know from personal experience how well self-reliance works. If it had worked, I wouldn't need A.A. I wouldn't need you.

Our Big Book describes this so well: "Selfishness – self-centeredness! That we think is the root of our troubles. Driven by a hundred forms of fear *(a hundred forms of fear!),* self-delusion, self-seeking, and self-pity, we step on the toes of others, and they retaliate. Sometimes they hurt us, seemingly without provocation, but we invariably find that at some time in the past, we have made decisions based on self which later placed us in a position to be hurt."

"Above everything, we alcoholics must be rid of this selfishness. We must, or it kills us." "God makes that possible. And there often seems no way of entirely getting rid of self without his aid."

"It is by dying that one awakens to eternal life." St. Francis' prayer is, of course, a spiritual objective, one way of seeking to *improve* my conscious contact with God. This prayer helps me to realize that I can only be a *channel* of this spiritual power, not the *source*. This awareness takes my ego out of the equation, and I can focus more on the other person. When I'm obsessed with me, me, me, I am full of fear. This is a direct denial of God's power in my life. You would think that my feelings of fear, anger, and frustration would be a good indication that I know somewhere inside me that I am incapable of controlling life's situations. Here is one of my favorite quotes from the Big Book: "We suffered under the delusion that we could wrest satisfaction and happiness out of this world if we only *managed* well."

Until I came into Alcoholics Anonymous and began to learn to look at life from an *entirely different angle,* I was convinced that if the hammer that I was using to force my will on others did not work—I needed a bigger hammer!

I was the ant floating downstream on a log, convinced that I was steering the log!

I look at Alcoholics Anonymous as God's schoolroom. Most of what I learn is unconscious, but it is the unconscious learning that changes and shapes my thinking and feeling.

Because of the *repetitious changes in my behavior,* everything else changes as well.

Throughout this personal exploration of my experience with the Traditions in my relationships, I've been talking about spiritual objectives as a cumulative way of improving my conscious contact with the God of my experience.

I can only do this *through my interactions with you.* My spiritual life does not center around my time at home alone in prayer and meditation, although that usually sets the tone for the day ahead. No, my spiritual life each day centers around how I treat every person who shows up on my path that day.

This self-centered drunk turned out to really *want* the serenity and peace that comes from seeking to become happy and usefully whole. The simple kit of spiritual tools that A.A. offers turns out not to be so complicated and daunting after all.

The real reason I incorporate the Twelve Steps and Twelve Traditions into my daily life can be summed up this way: I promised myself at the beginning that I would be continuously willing to go to any lengths to overcome my demon alcohol.

I *thought* I just came to A.A. to quit drinking. To my great astonishment, I discovered that alcohol was just a symptom of what was wrong with me: my real problem was that I suffered from a spiritual malady. Once I began to recover spiritually, I could recover mentally and physically. Imagine my surprise when I found that my primary goal in life is to be of maximum service to God and those about me. Who knew?

It really is about me, me, me, after all, but not in the way I believed when I first came to you.

"*Give time, time,*" my sponsor said when I was a new-comer. She continued to say this for the next forty years. Long before she died, I was not only saying this to myself, but I was also offering it to others in recovery (and some that were not!). It was the repetition, over time, that profoundly altered my habitual way of thinking about the world, the people in it, and me!

Of course, I was unaware that this was happening as I tried to remember to practice these principles in all my affairs: in 12-Step calls, with my home group members, my newfound friends in the women's meeting, unknown people in line at the bank, the clerk at the department store, the anonymous person driving *way* too slowly in front of me, and the person ahead of me with 21 items in the 20-item line at the grocery store.

Sometimes I would engage those anonymous people in conversation, and the result would usually be a joyful encounter. I found that almost everyone felt the same way! By the magic of a pleasant conversation, this hostility was defused in me *and* in them, and the *real* people came out to play!

Dealing with people I didn't know, I learned that I had been looking at and judging the outward *shell* of that person, not the soul that inhabited that body.

The **"Namaste"** effect occurred when I could say, "The spirit in me acknowledges and salutes the spirit in you."

Ultimately, and I think most importantly, I learned to exercise love and tolerance for those *closest* to me. This was the most challenging task because they were not casual or fleeting relationships – they were always *here!* They were here today, and they would be here tomorrow!

Alcoholics Anonymous is God's schoolroom. Everything in it can be looked at as a metaphor:

I *thought* I was just living with my alcoholic father during the very beginning of my sobriety – I was really learning to honor, respect, and love the *person* while I didn't love his *behavior*.

I *thought* I was just going to meetings – I was really learning how to become *teachable*.

I *thought* I was just saying my prayers – I was really learning how to become spiritually fit.

I *thought* I was just going to the business meetings of my home group – I was really learning acceptance, tolerance, and patience.

I *thought* I was taking care of business on a daily basis. I was really learning how to practice these principles in all my affairs.

I *thought* I was just a mother to my grown daughter. I was really learning that everyone, even grown children, has their own Higher Power and their own path to follow. How they carry out that journey is none of my business.

I *thought* I was gaining friendships – I was really learning that to have a friend, I have to be a friend. I wanted everyone to accept me the way I was; why shouldn't my friend count on the same love and tolerance I expect from her? I had to reach out to my friend; I had to be really interested in and concerned about *her* life as well as my own.

That "Love thy neighbor as thyself" thing took on a new significance as I sought to improve my conscious contact with the God of my ever-changing understanding.

I *thought* I was just getting married to husband #4 (Bill). I was really learning how to honor a 100% commitment and to live in the Steps and Traditions, especially the concept of **unity**, in order to have a healthy marriage. Through consistent, repetitive hard work on both our parts, my husband Bill and I achieved a spirit-based, other-centered, unselfish, principles-above-personalities relationship long before his death in 1997.

When Bill died suddenly and unexpectedly, I was immediately surrounded by the loving arms of my sponsor and all the friends and acquaintances I had taken the time and effort to nurture on this journey of recovery.

I especially remember when the women I sponsor called, saying, "I didn't want to call and bother you." I could truthfully say that the only time I wasn't in pain was when I was talking to them *about them* and thinking of someone else. I was momentarily *outside of myself* and my grief.

An important lesson in other-centeredness I use today.

And the beat goes on.

Life goes on.

And the story continues for every one of us every day.

Life is all about relationships, whether it's the man or woman in your life or the clerk at the grocery store. The more we practice the principles embedded in the A.A. program in *all* our relationships, the more we change, and the more our relationships change.

Not everyone wants to grow and change, and even among those who do, not everyone takes the actions required to do so. The monumental fact that you have completed this workbook means you are a seeker, a winner, and a genuinely sober person. It doesn't matter how long you've been in recovery – it's not years that count; it's *attitude and action!*

Mother Teresa, a beautiful, God-centered, loving, and tolerant non-alcoholic with an amazing *attitude*, says it this way:

"People are often unreasonable and
self-centered. Forgive them anyway.
If you are kind, people may accuse you of ulte-
rior motives. Be kind anyway.
If you are honest, people may cheat you.
Be honest anyway.
If you find happiness, people may be jealous.
Be happy anyway.
The good you do today may be forgotten
tomorrow. Do good anyway.
Give the world the best you have, and it may
never be enough. Give your best anyway.
For you see, in the end, it is between
you and God.
It was never between you and them anyway."

I hope you found this Workbook has somewhat answered the question ***"How do we get from Healing to Harmony?"*** I say "somewhat" because we will *always* be on this exciting learning journey.

I have a choice to make with every encounter, and today I choose to meet the world and the people in it as a happy, joyous and loving child of God.

As the poet Rumi says, "After all, we are just walking each other home."

Writing this workbook has been a beautiful and memorable experience in *my* journey of recovery, and I leave you with this:

The Spirit in me recognizes, respects, and loves the Spirit in you.

Namaste.

<br clear="all" />

Questions from
Tradition Twelve

Chapter Twelve

1. In my relationships, am I unselfishly concerned for the welfare of others? If not, why not?

2. Do I live my life by the principle of anonymity? Is this the same as humility? Is this the same as teachability?

3. Do I do something nice for someone every day and not let them know about it? Is this humility?

4. *Do I treat others with the same love and tolerance that God has treated me?*

   - *My husband/wife/child*
   - *My girlfriend/boyfriend*
   - *My neighbor*
   - *My friend/co-worker*
   - *The postman/grocery clerk*

5. *Have I learned to love the person while not liking their behavior?*

6. *What is my spiritual foundation? Is it the foundation upon which I build my daily life?*

7. *Do I feel I have put the Twelve Steps and Twelve Traditions inside of me so that they are my "go-to" in dealing with any relationship? Are they my first choice in responding to any situation?*

8. *In any relationship, do I listen to the message and not focus on the messenger, even if the messenger is (to me) obnoxious?*

9. Do I ever consider that I am the obnoxious personality that someone else has to overlook?

10. Do I practice love and tolerance towards myself as well as others? Do I beat myself up when I make a mistake?

11. Am I the best best? Am I the best worst? Do I acknowledge and respect my character assets?

12. Do I stick with the problem, or do I look for the solution?

13. If my goal is to fit myself to be of maximum service to God and the people around me, am I willing to go to any lengths to achieve this goal?

Fair Fighting

Conflicts inevitably arise in most relationships, and for many of us, they create significant discomfort. If handled appropriately, conflict can strengthen relationships and improve our understanding of each other. When handled badly, conflict can result in broken friendships, ended relationships, and long-simmering feuds.

This is an *overview* of the fair fighting rules. More details can be found in Tradition Three and on the Internet.

Fair Fighting Ground Rules:

1. Remain calm
2. Be specific about what is bothering you
3. Deal with only one issue at a time
4. No "hitting below the belt"
5. Avoid accusations
6. Don't generalize
7. Don't stockpile
8. Avoid clamming up
9. Establish common ground rules

Remember, the goal is not to "win" but to come to a mutually satisfying and peaceful solution to the problem.

Active Listening

PAY ATTENTION

    a) Look at the speaker directly.

    b) Put aside distracting thoughts.

    c) Don't mentally prepare a rebuttal.

    d) "Listen" to the speaker's body language.

SHOW THAT YOU'RE LISTENING

Use your own body language and gestures to show you're engaged

    a) Nod occasionally.

    b) Smile and use other facial expressions.

    c) Make sure your posture is open.

    d) Encourage the speaker to continue with small verbal comments.

PROVIDE FEEDBACK

Our personal filters, assumptions, judgments, and beliefs can distort what we hear. To understand what is being said, you might need to reflect on what is being said and ask questions.

    a) Paraphrase. "What I'm hearing is...."

       "Sounds like you're saying..." is a great way to reflect.

    b) Ask questions to clarify specific points: "What do you mean by...."

    c) Summarize the speaker's comments periodically.

    d) If you find yourself responding emotionally, say so. Ask for more information.

       "I may not be understanding you correctly, and I find myself taking what you said personally. What I thought you said is XXX. Is that what you meant?"

DEFER JUDGMENT

Interrupting is a waste of time. It frustrates the speaker and limits the complete understanding of the message.

    a) Allow the speaker to finish each point before asking questions.

    b) Don't interrupt with counterarguments.

RESPOND APPROPRIATELY

Active listening is designed to encourage respect and understanding. You add nothing by attacking the speaker and otherwise putting them down.

     a) Be candid, open, and honest in your response

     b) Assert your opinions respectfully.

     c) Treat the other person the way you would
        like to be treated.

ACKNOWLEDGMENT:

Active listening emerged from early 1940's research into what made an effective counselor. This enquiry was largely led by Carl Rogers and his colleagues

Caregiving/Caretaking

Care*taking* feels stressful, exhausting, irritating, and frustrating.
Care*giving* energizes and inspires.

Care*takers* cross boundaries.
Care*givers* honor boundaries.

Care*takers* take from the recipient and give with strings attached.
Care*givers* give freely.

Care*takers* don't practice self-care because they mistakenly believe it's a selfish act.
Care*givers* practice self-care because they know that keeping themselves happy enables them to be of service to others.

Care*takers* worry.
Care*givers* take action and solve problems.

Care*takers* think they know what's best for others.
Care*givers* only know what's best for themselves.

Care*takers* don't trust others' abilities to care for themselves.
Care*givers* trust others enough to allow them to activate their inner guidance and problem-solving capabilities.

Care*taking* creates anxiety and/or depression in the caretaker.
Care*giving* decreases anxiety and/or depression in the caregiver.

Care*takers* tend to attract needy people.
Care*givers* tend to attract people who want to be healthy.

Care*takers* tend to be judgmental.
Care*givers* practice a "live and let live" attitude.

Care*takers* start "fixing" when a problem arises for someone else.
Care*givers* empathize, letting others know they are not alone, and lovingly ask, "What are you going to do about that?"

Care*takers* start "fixing" when a problem arises.
Care*givers* respectfully wait to be asked to help.

Care*takers* tend to be dramatic in their caretaking and focus on the problem.

Care*givers* can create dramatic results by focusing on the solution.

Care*takers* use the word "You" a lot.

Care*givers* say "I" more.

As with changing any behavior, becoming aware is the first step. Watch yourself the next time you are with someone and ask yourself where you fall on the continuum.

Author: Elizabeth Kupferman, Licensed RN and Counselor in Texas

Care*takers* are judgmental, controlling, self-righteous and opinionated.

Care*givers* are none of those things. They practice A.A.'s code: "Love and tolerance of others."

By the way:

Care*takers* make lousy sponsors, encouraging those they sponsor to become overly dependent and not autonomous. Care*takers* will fire a sponsee if the sponsee displeases them by drinking or acting independently.

Care*givers* make **great** sponsors, encouraging and supporting those they sponsor to become responsible, emotionally sober grown-ups.

Characteristics of Adult Children of Alcoholics or Other Dysfunctional families

We became isolated and afraid of people and authority figures.

We became approval seekers and lost our identity in the process.

We are frightened by angry people and any personal criticism.

We either became alcoholics, married them, or both, or found another compulsive personality, such as a workaholic, to fulfill our sick abandonment needs.

We live life from the viewpoint of victims and are attracted by that weakness in our love and friendship relationships.

We have an overdeveloped sense of responsibility, and it is easier for us to be concerned with others rather than ourselves; this enables us not to look too closely at our own faults, etc.

We feel guilty when we stand up for ourselves instead of giving in to others.

We become addicted to excitement.

We confuse love and pity and tend to 'love" people we can "pity" and "rescue."

We have "stuffed" our feelings from our traumatic childhoods and have difficulty feeling or expressing our feelings because it hurts so much (Denial).

We judge ourselves harshly and have a shallow sense of self-esteem.

We are dependent personalities who are terrified of abandonment and will do anything to hold onto a relationship in order not to experience the painful feelings of abandonment that we received from living with sick people who were never there emotionally for us.

Alcoholism is a family disease; we became para-alcoholics and took on the characteristics of that disease even though we did not pick up the drink.

Para-alcoholics are reactors rather than actors.

Adult Children of Alcoholics/Dysfunctional Families World Service Organization, Inc. "The Laundry List"

Boundaries

Boundaries are about social interaction – taking necessary action to protect and care for ME in a healthy way without overstepping YOUR boundaries. Healthy boundaries are essential for physical, emotional, and spiritual health. They may be different for each person and each relationship, and boundaries may change over time.

Basic Characteristics:

1. Expect respect – it's a fundamental right.
2. Communicate – I must say what I need.
3. Don't overexplain – "No" is a complete sentence.
4. Establish consequences – I must explain why it's important to me, keep the focus on me, and be willing to follow through if the boundary is violated.

There are many good books, podcasts, and videos about Boundaries on the internet and in our libraries.

References

ALCOHOLICS ANONYMOUS FOURTH EDITION; New and revised 2001

TWELVE STEPS AND TWELVE TRADITIONS; Copyright 1952, 1953 by the A.A. Grapevine, Inc. Twelfth Printing; June 1973

COURAGE TO CHANGE: Al-Anon Family Groups, al-anon.org.

THE FOUR AGREEMENTS: a practical guide to personal freedom; Copyright 1997 by Miguel Angel Ruiz, M.D.

DAVE RAMSEY: Total Money Makeover; Classic edition

CARETAKING VS. CAREGIVING; Author: Elizabeth Kupferman, Licensed R.N. and Counselor in Texas

FIVE KEY LISTENING SKILLS: Mind Tools; mindtools.com
Active listening emerged from early 1940s research into what made an effective counselor. This inquiry was primarily led by Carl Rogers and his colleagues.

"THE LAUNDRY LIST": Adult Children of Alcoholics/ Dysfunctional Families World Service Organization, Inc.

FAIR FIGHTING: Therapist Aid; Woody Schuldt, LMHC

BOUNDARIES: Loveisrespect.org

These are just some of the references for each of the categories I have written about concerning healthy/ unhealthy relationships. Many more are to be found on the Internet and in Libraries.

About the Author

Rena K. has spent almost half a century learning how to be "sober" in the true sense of the word. Early in recovery, she realized she knew how to have relationships – but didn't know how to have healthy relationships. So, with the guidance of many wise people, she resolutely turned the spotlight on herself to learn the skills and attitudes necessary to enjoy healthy, happy relationships.

This memoir/workbook is not just a collection of stories but a practical guide based on her personal experiences, the wisdom of sponsors, and the occasional professional. It's a vulnerable account of how she has learned and applied these tools for over four decades—in all areas of her life!

Rena currently lives in South Florida and loves her sober life! She is passionate about Alcoholics Anonymous, the privilege of sponsorship, the joy of fellowship, and the excitement of both attending and sharing her experience, strength, and hope at conferences around the world.

When she is at home, she enjoys spending time with her husband, Cole, and her friends both in and out of A.A. And writing.

You can find Rena K. at recoveryandmore.info or reach her by email at info@recoveryandmore.info

Made in the USA
Middletown, DE
08 September 2024

60478806R00205